Translating Institutions

An Ethnographic Study of EU Translation

Kaisa Koskinen

St. Jerome Publishing

Manchester, UK & Kinderhook (NY), USA

Published by
St. Jerome Publishing
2 Maple Road West, Brooklands
Manchester, M23 9HH, United Kingdom
Telephone +44 (0)161 973 9856
Fax +44 (0)161 905 3498
stjerome@compuserve.com
http://www.stjerome.co.uk

InTrans Publications
P. O. Box 467
Kinderhook, NY 12106, USA
Telephone (518) 758-1755
Fax (518) 758-6702

ISBN 978-1-905763-08-5 (pbk)

Printed and bound in Great Britain by
T. J. International Ltd, Cornwall, UK

Typeset by
Delta Typesetters, Cairo, Egypt
Email: hilali1945@yahoo.co.uk

British Library Cataloguing in Publication Data
A catalogue record of this book is available from the British Library

Library of Congress Cataloging in Publication Data
Koskinen, Kaisa.
  Translating institutions : an ethnographic study of EU translation / Kaisa Koskinen.
      p. cm.
  Includes bibliographical references and index.
  ISBN 978-1-905763-08-5 (pbk. : alk. paper)
1. Translating and interpreting--Social aspects. 2. European Commission--Translating services. I. Title.
  P306.97.S63K67 2008
  418'.02094--dc22
                              2008002362

Translation is the language of Europe.

Umberto Eco

Translating Institutions

An Ethnographic Study of EU Translation

Kaisa Koskinen

Translating Institutions aims to provide a framework for research on translation in institutional settings, using the Finnish translation unit at the European Commission as a case study. Because of their foundational multilingualism, the institutions of the European Union could be described as both transla*ting* and transla*ted* institutions. The European Commission alone employs nearly two thousand translators, and it is translators who draft the vast majority of outgoing EU messages. *Translating Institutions* sets out to explore the organizational role and professional identity of this group of cultural mediators, a group that has remained relatively invisible despite its size and central institutional role, and to use the analysis of this data to elaborate broader methodological and theoretical issues.

Translating Institutions adopts an ethnographic approach to explore the life and work of the translators at the centre of this study. In practice, this entails employing a number of different methods and interrogating various types of data. The three-level research design used covers the study of the *institutional framework*, the study of *translators* working in specific institutional settings, and the study of translated *documents* and their source texts. This is therefore a study of *both* texts *and* people in their institutional habitat. Given the methodological focus of the volume, the different methods and data are outlined in independent chapters: the institutional framework of translation (institutional ethnography), the physical location of the unit (observation), translators' own views of their role (focus group discussions), and a sociologically-oriented text analysis of a sample document (shifts analysis).

Translating Institutions constitutes a valuable contribution to the sociology of translation. It opens up new avenues for research and offers a detailed framework for the study of institutional translation.

Kaisa Koskinen is Lecturer and Adjunct Professor at the School of Modern Languages and Translation Studies, University of Tampere, Finland. She is author of *Beyond Ambivalence: Postmodernity and the Ethics of Translation* (2000) and various articles that examine theoretical and methodological questions in translation studies, retranslation, translation in the European Union, and the ethics of translation. Her interest in EU translation stems from her previous insider role as a translator working for the European Commission.

Table of Contents

Acknowledgements

Writing this book has been quite a journey for me – mentally, geographically and institutionally. Several people have assisted me along the way, or travelled by my side.

I want to thank Christina Schäffner (Aston University), Şebnem Susam-Sarajeva (University of Edinburgh) and Andrew Chesterman (University of Helsinki) for giving me opportunities to present and discuss the project in its early phases. I am also greatly indebted to Mona Baker and the anonymous reviser whose insightful comments were invaluable to me during the final steps: the remaining shortcomings are due to my inabilities in following their advice.

Travelling into the territories of the social sciences was made both safer and more fun by a group of social scientists: warm thanks to all my fellow fellows in the University of Tampere Centre for Advanced Study (2004-2005). The daily lunches we shared prove that it indeed matters who you eat with!

Numerous colleagues at the Department of Translation Studies in the School of Modern Languages and Translation Studies (University of Tampere) have given me enormous help with their discussions, comments and revisions: I wish to thank them all. I owe a huge thank you to Kate Moore for her help with English.

During each journey, there are moments when you are homesick and the suitcase feels too heavy. This journey has not been an exception. I am particularly grateful to Lea Henriksson and Kristiina Abdallah, not only for their insights into the methods and content of this book, but also, and in particular, for their unfailing support during the highs and lows of my journey. Outi Paloposki has walked by my side throughout this journey, and through my entire academic itinerary: I cannot thank her enough.

This journey begins and ends in Luxembourg. I wish to thank the European Commission institutionally and Emma Wagner, Marja Kalliopuska, Erkka Vuorinen and Jyrki Lappi-Seppälä personally for making this research possible. The Finnish translators in the European Commission, the *sine qua non* of this study, remain anonymous here. But my greatest gratitude is to them, to their willingness to share their life with me, and with the readers of this book. It is to them, and to all anonymous and invisible institutional translators, that I dedicate this book.

1. Introduction

1.1 Net-weaving

On a late autumn day in 1756, a peasant girl called Liisa was herding cows in the forest of Santtio, in Southwestern Finland, when she had a vision of God's anger. Terrified, she ran to the village to preach repentance. This was the beginning of an ecstatic revivalist movement that spread all over the Western coast of Finland. In the 1990s, the historian Irma Sulkunen got interested in Liisa, only to find out that little was known of this person who gave such an impetus to the religious life of the era. Sulkunen soon discovered that there are very few historical facts available; it cannot even be confirmed that Liisa actually ever existed. Some official records indicate that there were several Liisas of the same age group (this is a common name in Finland), but there is no way of knowing for sure whether she was one of them (Sulkunen 1999). Sulkunen discovered that from the perspective of the present-day historian Liisa was invisible. Sulkunen has later explained that in order to make Liisa visible, she had to use a particular method: through a microhistorical close reading and collective biography she started weaving a net around Liisa. Sulkunen thought that if she could only weave a tight net of the surrounding community, in the end the net would have a hole the size of Liisa in it (Sulkunen 2003).

Microhistory is the study of history on a small scale. Case studies, such as Sulkunen's study of Liisa and her context, typically focus on an individual, a particular incident or on a small community. Through their small object of study, however, microhistories often have great ramifications, revealing larger structures by way of a detailed analysis of the individual case. Throughout her research career, Sulkunen has concentrated most on those who are not in the limelight: women in the shadow of men, ordinary people not found in history books, and those whose political views were at their time overruled by their contemporaries. She has taken it as her task to bring to light those who have remained in the dark.

Translators are often seen to live a similar 'shadowy' existence; the history of translation has been described as the study of a shadow culture (*Schattenkultur*) (Kittel 1998[1]). But the method of net weaving can also be used to make translators more visible. The tighter the net we weave, the more clearly we can discern the translator in the middle. The net can be woven into the past, to reconstruct a historical context, but it makes even more sense to do the weaving contemporaneously, collecting the data – i.e. raw material for weaving – as events unfold. This ethnographic research model is based on a

---

[1] I am grateful to Pekka Kujamäki for bringing this reference to my attention.

comprehensive approach, where the researcher/weaver puts the object of study as the nexus and makes use of all kinds of material to grasp all the relevant connecting lines that form the net around it.

Sulkunen's metaphor of net-weaving captures a particular ethos of research. This way of observing is contextualizing and situated. As such, it also accommodates complexity and contradictory evidence. This approach thus bears family resemblance to another methodology, what is referred to as the nexus model and proposed by Joanne Martin (2002) for the study of organization cultures (see also Chapter 3). This nexus model is based on accepting ambiguities and multiple ties in a person's cultural identifications. Instead of trying to fix a solid interpretation of the culture of a particular organization, the nexus approach takes the organization as its starting point and begins to chart the various points of identification and connection around it. In short, the nexus orientation is based on weaving a net of identifications.

1.2 The European Commission as a translated institution

This study will also weave a net around a particular community – the Finnish translators working at the European Commission in Luxembourg. They are the nexus of this study. With the help of an ethnographic approach, I will try to make visible and comprehensible how these translators orient to their institutional setting and how they perceive their role as mediators between the institution and the outside world. In order to make the shape and silhouette of the translators discernible, they will be seen against the background of the institutional and material context of their work. This approach is therefore predominantly institutional: I am interested in seeing how this particular institutional context moulds the translation processes and how the translators negotiate their role and professional identity. Moreover, I am also interested in investigating how and whether these processes and identifications are reflected in the translations themselves.

In today's world, a sizeable number of translations are produced in different institutions, in international and supranational organizations such as the European Union or the United Nations, in government institutions of bilingual or multilingual countries, and in the public services of our increasingly hybridized and multicultural societies. These institutional contexts are, of course, numerous and varied, but they also share fundamental similarities: the translations are constrained and controlled by the translating institution, and the official nature of the institution endows the documents with authority and performative power. In order to understand and critically appreciate the translations produced in these settings, it is necessary to comprehend the dynamics of institutional language work as well as the constructive and constraining influence of the institutional context. As it is the institutional ideologies that provide the framework and basis for translation work, changes in these ideologies can fundamentally reshape the conditions of work. For example, Brian Mossop's recent article (2006) provides ample evidence as to how the repercussions of a shift in the institutional philosophy from a predominantly cultural to an economic logic have affected the work routines and work organization in the Federal Translation Bureau in Canada.

In order to understand the textual work carried out in institutional settings, one needs to have an understanding of the institution. Conversely, to understand these institutions, it is likewise necessary to comprehend the ways in which they are *textually* produced and reproduced. *Translating Institutions*, the title of this book, thus has two meanings: I will present a case study of *a translating institution* (the European Commission), but I also wish to emphasize that in their translations, the translators working for these institutions are in fact translating the institution itself (see Chapter 2). In a fundamental way, the European Union is a *translated institution*.

The European Union is, of course, also an interpreted institution. Although some parallels can be drawn for interpreting, this area largely remains outside the scope of this study. Contrary to Brian Mossop's (1988) claim that most interpretation is non-institutional, and that professional conference interpretation is an exceptional case, I would argue that institutional aspects are just as important in interpreting (community interpreting in particular) as they are in translating. But since the dynamics of translating and interpreting are not identical, and the institutional role of interpreters is not similar to that of translators, the Commission interpreters will not be included in this study. Within the European Union institutions, these two professions are also kept separate institutionally, with a separate organizational structure for both, and no posts for translator-interpreters available (for more on interpreting in EU settings, see Vuorikoski 2004).

The continuing globalization, growing co-operation and contact between cultures have increased the need for institutional translation and interpreting in both supranational and national contexts, but the translating and translated institutions as such have a long history. In fact, both writing and translating first took place in institutional settings. This dates back to the earliest writing systems which were exclusively used by the professional scribes working in the palaces or temples, in the service of secular or religious powers. For instance, early Sumerian, Mykenean, Egyptian, Mayan and Chinese texts were mainly either bureaucratic documents such as word lists for book-keeping or, later, political or religious propaganda. In contrast, the non-professional personal and poetic uses of writing are a later innovation (Diamond 2003: 252-253). In a similar manner, antecedents of today's intergovernmental institutions can be found in classical multicultural empires, with their interplay between *lingua francas* and local vernaculars. For example, Anthony Pym (2001: 2) draws parallels between the European Union institutions and the Holy Roman Empire of 926-1806:

> In Europe, the largely cultural Holy Germanic Empire might be one kind of background for the use of translation such as we find it in the European Union institutions, where the central political figure is traditionally weak, much decision-making power remains with the major nation-states and with their preferred languages, and translation foregrounds the symbolic plurality of those languages.

Considering the central role of translating – and translated – institutions throughout history, their relative absence in the theoretical discussions of translation is striking. Already in the late 1980s, Brian Mossop (1988:65) called for an institutional approach to translation and defined translating institutions as "a missing factor in translation theory". Apart from Mossop's own contributions (e.g., 2000, 2006), his call has remained largely unanswered, in particular beyond the field of literary translation where the role of the publishing houses and other institutions has received some attention, albeit mainly in historical case studies. And while since then there has been growing interest in translating in various institutional contexts such as the European Union, little more than sporadic articles and practitioners' own reflections on their work has been published (see, for example, Wagner et al. 2002, Tosi 2003; also Koskinen 2000a). These are valuable as such but different from a focused, research-oriented perspective. While trying not to lose touch with the insights gathered by practical experience, this book aims to bring together a number of theoretical considerations and empirical data relevant to institutional translation. The aim is to provide an overall framework for future research on translation in institutional settings. The overall objective is therefore to offer methodological guidelines on how to proceed – or how not to proceed if the reader wishes to choose a different path from those selected here.

The case study of institutional translation represented here focuses on the Finnish translation unit of the European Commission situated in Luxembourg. For a Finnish researcher, selecting the Finnish translation unit for a case study is a convenient choice,[2] but it also has wider implications. As a

---

[2] It is also convenient from the point of view of access. Gaining access to a research site is often a major obstacle in ethnographic studies of organizations, and selecting a site that is already familiar can crucially facilitate access. I had no trouble with getting the permissions needed to carry out my research, and I am convinced that my previous participant role as one of the employees in the same unit had a role in paving my way – although, contrary to a common presumption, the Commission is quite open to research proposals, and actually welcomes researchers (see, e.g., Wagner et al. 2002: 42).

non-Indo-European language, Finnish can be used as an 'acid test' for the translatability of texts or new terms (Lappi-Seppälä, cited in Wagner et al. 2002: 132). And as a 'small', non-procedural language within the Commission, Finnish represents the majority of the official languages, and joins ranks with all the new languages of the 2004 and 2007 enlargements, none of which can hope to achieve a 'working language' status. There is thus reason to believe that Finnish can function as a typical and telling example.

It is, however, somewhat difficult to communicate one's findings of the textual material in Finnish to an international readership who cannot be expected to know the language. This ironic difficulty in widening the perspective of translation studies outside the well-known European languages has been discussed by Michael Cronin (2003: 149). Cronin laments the tendency of researchers like myself coming from different 'minority language' backgrounds to avoid the problems of explaining the linguistic and cultural specificity of our data by resorting to more general discussions. To some extent that strategy will be applied here as well, but I will also try to convey the 'Finnishness' of my case, in spite of the unavoidable translation process of my data (field notes, questionnaire, interview material), and the readers' potential need to take my interpretations of the Finnish translations for granted.

While Finnish is, and will remain, a small language in the context of the EU institutions, EU translations are not a small issue in the Finnish context. Entry to the European Union has had a great and continuing impact on the job markets of Finnish translators and interpreters, not only by offering a relatively large number of permanent, well-paid jobs for in-house translators and interpreters but also by providing (both directly and indirectly via increased EU-wide business contacts) a steady flow of work to quite a number of freelancers. For a country of five million inhabitants, the hundreds of new job opportunities that opened in and prior to the year 1995 changed the field of translation quite dramatically. Since many of the new Member States are even smaller in size than Finland, similar changes they undergo may well have an even more dramatic effect. This has already been implied in the difficulty for the EU institutions to recruit the 135 new translators they would need per language from countries such as Estonia (1.4 million), or Slovenia (2 million), not to mention Malta (400,000 inhabitants).

1.3 Ethnography: a weaving method

Weaving a comprehensive net around institutional translation requires a variety of perspectives. The first step towards understanding why institutional translations are the way they are is to define not only what they are like but also how they came into being that way. One therefore needs to analyze not only the end product but also the process behind it. But neither the product nor the production process makes much sense unless they are studied in relation to the overall institutional setting that shapes and directs them. However, it can also be argued that the institutional setting is not a pre-existing structure: it only comes into being as a consequence of the everyday actions of the people who inhabit it. In an important manner, since they are *textually* produced and reproduced in their everyday text flow, the translating institutions are largely produced and reproduced *in and by translations*. An institution that relies on translations for its communication also relies on translators who play a crucial role in the successes and failures of its multilingual communication.

These multiple perspectives require methodological flexibility. In this book, methodological and theoretical insights adopted will be collected from a wide array of disciplines, from sociology and organization theory to cultural studies and anthropology. The three-level design used here includes the study of the *institutional framework*, the study of *translators* working in these institutional settings, and the study of translated *documents* and their source texts. This is a study of **both** texts **and** people in their institutional habitat.

The design is held together by an overall ethnographic approach. Ethnography allows for using multiple sources of data, multiple methods of analysis, and for multiple sites and time-frames. Ethnography pays equal attention to the minute details of everyday experience and to the structures and forces that bear on them. In the following chapters, the perspective changes from the study of the overall institutional framework and physical settings to an analysis of the translators' discourses, and an analysis of the shifts in a case document and its translation. What remains constant is the ethnographic orientation: the institutional framework is analyzed from an ethnographic perspective on organizational culture; data collection in focus group interviews, the questionnaire and observations are ethnographically oriented; and the text documents are perceived as being artefacts of a particular culture and interpreted against the background of the cultural framework where they originated. Ethnographic orientation as it is understood here provides a loose methodological framework and ethos for the research process. This ethnographic stance entails a commitment to an open-ended research process; ethnography aims at understanding a social phenomenon by making sense of it through engaged observation and in-depth explanation. It is a dialogic combination of different viewpoints, those of the observer and those of the observed, and a combination of different kinds of data, those elicited and those occurring naturally.

1.4 Small is beautiful

Ethnography is a comprehensive methodology. This is precisely why it is so appealing, but it also leaves it vulnerable to criticism. It is easy enough to point out all the different levels and aspects that need to be studied. It is simple to claim that we need to take into account both the micro and macro levels, paying attention to their interdependencies, and that it is also necessary that we analyze both texts and their producers, not overlooking the processes. Yet this is easier said than done. The ultimate challenge lies in integrating the perspectives into a meaningful and manageable entity. Multilingual institutions are almost by definition complex (the need to operate in several languages causing unavoidable complexity), as are multifaceted research designs. It has been argued that "a complete description of IBM would take the lifelong efforts of a substantial number of researchers" (Czarniawska-Joerges 1992: 186). There is no reason to believe that complex translated institutions would be much easier or quicker to study. It follows that research projects have to be narrowed down considerably; in a one-person research project with limited resources, one cannot make a comparative analysis of all aspects of institutional translation in the numerous different contexts and languages.

The empirical case described in this book is a result of this process of narrowing: the field of institutional translation was narrowed down to the EU institutions – perceived as a prototype case of an institutional setting – which was subsequently narrowed down to the European Commission and further to the Finnish translation units, and finally to the Luxembourg unit. The actual samples are drawn from the work flow of that particular unit: I followed the textual trail of the drafting process of one document, and I observed and interviewed the translators for one week. Compared to the size of the overall field, the samples that I study are microscopic. One document and one week represent a minuscule fraction of the work flow of even that one unit, no to mention the entire field of institutional translation. Yet this is a conscious methodological choice, based on the beauty of smallness and the value of multiple viewpoints. By focusing on a detailed analysis of small samples it is, I trust, possible to increase our understanding of the larger whole the samples were abstracted from. And by keeping the sample sizes reasonable, it is possible to accommodate several kinds of data and methods. Further, there already exist several general introductions to the language work in the EU institutions (e.g., an insider view by Wagner *et al.* 2002, and an outsider view by Phillipson 2003: Ch. 4), but little is known of the everyday workings of the translation services.

Continuing with the microscope metaphor, one could compare the method of narrowing down to laboratory analysis. The specific document used in this study (see Chapter 6) is extracted from the text flow (and the one week from the work flow) in a manner similar to taking a sample of river water in a test tube. The validity of this analysis then largely depends on how representative the sample is. Institutional text production can be described as a relatively stable, controlled, or standardized, and normative form of activity. For this reason it is safe to assume that the analysis of individual texts can open up important vistas to the general field of the institutional production of meaning (Heikkinen *et al.* 2000: 11). The recent boom of corpus studies in TS has undoubtedly brought new insights into the processes that take place in translation, and this increased interest in corpus analysis has enabled research designs that would be unthinkable without the help of modern technology. But parallel to the resulting emphasis on quantification and large corpora it is, I think, necessary not to lose sight of the value of detailed case studies. In an excellent article on research methods, and on the virtues of using metaphoric microscopes and telescopes in research, Maria Tymoczko suggests that we work "toward the macroscopic from the direction of the microscopic, or vice versa, so that one's data from the macroscopic level are complemented and confirmed by data from the microscopic level" (2002: 17). I hope that by putting together the results of the microscopic analysis and of a 'telescopic' view of the landscape of the translation policy implemented by the European Commission, I will be able to offer an advanced understanding of EU translation.

1.5 Role of the researcher

Traditional ethnographic research in anthropology would require a lengthy period (perhaps several years) of participant observation, and short visits to the field have been described as mere ethnographic tourism (e.g. Eipper 1998). In this study, as in many contemporary ethnographic projects, the logic adopted is different. Instead of a long, participant observation period, this research is based on an initial phase of 'observant participation'. A significant background factor in this project is related to my own personal history: I first entered the field of EU translation not as a researcher but among the first wave of Finnish staff translators recruited into the (then) Translation Service of the European Commission after Finland's accession in 1995. I arrived at the Luxembourg Unit in May, 1996, and left for first maternity leave and then for a leave of absence in November 1997. This period of actually *being* an insider has provided a basis for my later work, both facilitating my (re-)entry to the field and supporting the research design and analysis of my later 'tourism' in the same locale. Although I have not actually worked in my functionary capacity since, I only resigned from my office in 2002, which means that for a large part of my research project (carried out intermittently in 1999-2006), I was a 'double agent', partially an insider, partially an outsider. Through all these years I have also kept at least sporadically in touch with some of my former colleagues, but visited Luxembourg only in my researcher role.

Contrary to regular laments of a rift between theory and practice, many translation scholars do have experience in practical translation work, and it is not uncommon for them to build on this experience in their research. Combining the two is not, however, straightforward. This is because personal experience is an asset in research, but it also poses risks and difficulties. This experience may result in split loyalties to your colleagues in your working life on the one hand and to your academic objectivity on the other. The tacit knowledge acquired by first-hand experience is often difficult to integrate in research reports. Furthermore, there may be a conflict of roles. It is standard academic practice that a scholar cannot accept any opinion from the field at face value; any statement has to be subjected to further investigation. But what if one is both an informant and a scholar? For instance, as a scholar, can I trust myself as a translator? And then of course, there is the time factor: to what extent is the field still the same as it was when I left? How valid, or outdated, is my experience? It seems that analyzing a familiar professional activity requires an extra dose of self-reflexivity: one has to be ready to question one's own interpretations and to refrain from blindly trusting one's own insider knowledge. Because of its fundamental situatedness, ethnographic research opens up a range of possible researcher positions, from a completely detached observer to an undercover researcher in participant roles; it also offers a sustained framework for reflecting on the risks and benefits of the chosen position. This approach therefore also offers systematic ways of capitalizing on the experience of practitioners in translation studies.

Ethnography always contains a particular mix of voices. Throughout this book, dialogue takes place between the outsider and insider viewpoints. The translators' own voices enter into a discussion with a more detached analysis, and my personal memories enrich and balance my analytic academic discourse. This dialogue inevitably includes some tensions; tensions arise between explicit and implicit culture (between what is said and what is done), between the natives' voice and the researcher's voice (both within me, and between me and my informants), as well as between the local cultural world and the larger context (Schwartzman 1993: 72). There is, nonetheless, a conscious preference towards the insider view, resulting from the overall ethnographic ethos of the work. Ethnography, a method for grasping 'the native's point of view' (see Malinowski 1922) entails a basic orientation towards understanding the field one is studying from the perspective of those who inhabit it:

> One of the defining characteristics of ethnographic research is that the investigator goes into the field, instead of bringing the field to the investigator. Ethnographers go into the field to learn about a culture from the inside out. (Schwartzman 1993: 3-4)

The research process behind the present book has been cyclical in the sense of returning to and reshaping the research questions and complementing the initial understandings with new kinds of data and new ways of analysis: the first participation period and the resulting general observations (Koskinen

2000a) gave rise to a textual analysis of the actual texts (see Chapter 6), and these two were then put together with the results of group discussions (Chapter 5) and observations from the field (Chapter 4). The translators involved in the process have also had a chance to read all the relevant sections of the manuscript, and to give their comments on my interpretations.

1.6 The logic of both/and

The mixed insider/outsider researcher role applied in this study is not accidental. Rather, it is in line with the overall logic of the work. Throughout the project, the research design has been based on a conscious refusal to force a unified perspective on the object under study. The overriding principle in adopting a nexus, or net-weaving, approach has been to try to respect the complexity and richness of real life, to adopt a logic of both/and rather than submitting to choices of either/or. So, this is a study of both texts and people, both the text production process and the product, and both the micro level individuals as well as the institutional macro structure around them.

This logic of both/and connects the present project to my previous work on deconstruction and translation (e.g., Koskinen 1994; 2000b). If there is a lesson to be learned from deconstruction, it is surely that it sensitizes you to the need to question any simplified and binary representations, and urges you to embrace the messy and incongruent ambivalence of human life and to make the effort to account for that complexity. Instead of neatly categorizable patterns we often encounter contradictions, paradoxes and changing scenes. There is, in all research, a built-in logic of bringing order to the unruly practice, of forcing an interpretation on the infinite number of incongruent details one can abstract from any empirical data. The logic of both/and is a useful reminder that they are precisely that: *created* order and *forced* interpretations of a complex reality. Even so, the orderly interpretation is, however, a necessary creation, if we want to gain an understanding of anything, in research or in every-day life. Otherwise we might become paralyzed by the endless ambivalence:

> If we want to start something, we must ignore that our starting point is, *all efforts taken*, shaky. If we want to get something done, we must ignore that, *all provisions made*, the end will be inconclusive. This ignoring is not active forgetfulness; it is, rather, an active marginalizing of the marshiness, the swampiness, the lack of firm grounding in the margins, at beginning and end. (Spivak 1999: 175; italics in the original)

I am very much aware of the lack of firm grounding in the margins of my samples. Even though an effort has been made to include and explore a rich variety of factors related to translation in institutional settings, many more remain outside the scope of this study. Ethnography can never be conclusive; its data never gets saturated. The net is an appropriate metaphor for research because it allows for the incompleteness for which all research is always destined. By definition, nets have holes. The net I weave in this book is unavoidably riddled, but I hope it is tight enough to encourage others to weave their own nets.

1.7 Aims and structure of the book

This book is divided into two separate parts. Part I, containing Chapters 2 and 3, is a general theoretical and methodological introduction. Chapter 2 clarifies the basic concepts of institutions and institutional translation used in this book, and Chapter 3 is a general introduction to ethnographic methods. Part II offers a practical example of how these methods could be applied to the study of translators and translations. Three subsequent chapters include an analysis of the role and status of translators in official documents and ethnographic observations of the physical settings (Chapter 4), an analysis of the focus group discussions of the Finnish translators (Chapter 5), and a comparative study of source texts and translations (Chapter 6). Taken together, these three chapters offer a variety of vantage points for the work of the Finnish translators in the European Commission. In the final chapter, the resulting net will be assessed. Hopefully, the net will be tight enough to catch some fish.

This book has a strong methodological component. Its focus is on introducing ethnographic methods, this far little used in translation studies. The role of the case study is both to provide insight into EU translation and also to illustrate how these methods can be applied. For this reason, Chapters 4 to 6 also include information on methods so that they can be read independently, without relying on the general background explicated in Chapter 3: for example, the reader interested in the drafting process can go directly to Chapter 6, and the reader willing to learn about the use of focus groups can turn to Chapter 5.

The rationale behind this hands-on approach to methodology is my contention that we can only assess the usefulness of particular methodological frameworks by testing them in real situations. I hope to be able to demonstrate how ethnographic methods can be fruitfully applied in translation studies. Abstract 'how to' books on research methodology tend to depict an ideal world of flawless research designs, and can sometimes set dishearteningly high standards. In real-life research with its limited resources and unexpected drawbacks these standards can seldom be attained. When this tendency that is manifest in methodological guide books is combined with the emphasis on methods across disciplines in contemporary academia in general, and with the repeatedly expressed worries of a lack of methodological rigour in translation studies in particular,[3] new scholars entering the field will meet expectations far beyond those that were set for the previous generation of academics. I do agree that there is always a need to discuss methods on a general level, and to reflect on the solidity of one's own research practice on a more pragmatic level, but it is also important to remember that methods are just tools, not ends in themselves. In order to avoid a paralyzing effect of just introducing yet another complex set of methodological tools, I wanted to choose a pragmatic approach: in addition to introducing one methodological option available to aspiring scholars of the sociology of translation, this book tells an illustrative story of how and to what extent the principles of ethnography were applied in one particular case study that was actually conducted.

If detached from actual research praxis, methodology guide books can appear rather stiff and mechanical. Yet the reality of doing research calls for flexibility, intuition, improvising, prioritizing, and openness to new opportunities as they arise during the research process. Barbara Czarniawska-Joerges (1992: 113) expresses this succinctly by stating the following:

> The moral is to hold tightly to your (research) values and to make your methods flexible. Each situation and each organization requires adaptation and specific understanding. It is a pathetic enterprise to confront them with stiff research principles, laboriously elaborated in one's office.

---

[3] See, for example, Gile (1998). For a constructive criticism of the quality of research papers in TS, see Gile and Hansen (2004).

Part I
Theory and Methodology

2. Translating Institutions and Institutional Translation

2.1 Institutions

The term 'institution' is a slippery concept. In the social sciences and in everyday conversations institution can have a range of meanings: for instance, it can be used to refer to concrete physical institutions (say, the Smithsonian Institution), to 'total' institutions such as prisons or mental hospitals, to social institutions like the family, or to official posts (such as the president, or the Pope) – or it can be used as a handy way of expressing admiration and durable value: "the Rolling Stones is an institution". In academic discourse, the variety of usage is at least partially explained by the central status of the concept in sociological theories. In fact, when the new discipline of sociology first emerged in the late 19th century, it was defined as "the science of institutions" (Émile Durkheim, as cited in Merton 2001: xi). Since then, institutions have been studied, and the concept redefined, not only in sociology but also in, for example, economics, political science and organization studies. The concept of the institution has therefore proved to be fruitful and versatile, but it follows that it is also notoriously difficult to employ because of the possibilities of misunderstanding and confusion:

> Much of the challenge posed by this subject [of institutions and organizations] – to the author as well as the readers – resides in the many varying meanings and usages of the concept of institution. Being one of the oldest and most oft-employed ideas in social thought, it has continued to take on new and diverse meanings over time, much like barnacles on a ship's hull, without shedding the old. (Scott 2001: xx)

In this chapter, I try to spell out which meanings and usages are evoked in this book. I will first present an overview of how institutions have been seen in the social sciences, and then narrow the focus to the relations between institutions and translation. These relations can be found and studied on a number of levels. I do not want to give the impression of 'shedding' some approaches, because this is not an evaluation exercise designed to dictate which usages are acceptable in translation studies and which are not. Nevertheless, since the twin concepts of 'institution' and 'institutional' play such a central role in this book, it is necessary to be explicit about which meanings are attached to institutions in this context, and especially about those which are not. For other research purposes, the choice could be different.

In the abundant literature on institutions, explicit definitions of how institutions are understood in particular studies are surprisingly rare, and the taken-for-granted definitions often need to be distilled from the details of the analysis or judged by the choice of prominent names that are referred to. In the following, I try to outline a very general, and necessarily simplified, picture of the main trends. Sociology has had a long tradition of exploring 'social institutions', that is, symbolic systems of knowledge, belief and moral authority that guide our behaviour in all human interaction (Scott 2001: 13). These systems, it has been argued, are based on social norms and normative control (see, in particular, Parsons 1967). In other words, norms are an essential part of each society, and by studying norms one can understand a culture. Recently, this approach, which is referred to as control theory approach (i.e., the view that our action is controlled by social norms), has often been replaced by a constructivist framework, emphasizing the creation of shared knowledge and co-construction of meanings and beliefs rather than rules and norms (see Alasuutari 2004: Ch. 2). According to the constructivist view, social institutions (such as parenting, giving and accepting gifts, ways of greeting...) are not pre-existing structures but are only socially constructed, or enacted, in human interaction.

Alongside the traditional emphasis on all-encompassing social institutions, on which both the control theory approach and the constructivist approach are based, there are two distinct fields of study where institutions are defined somewhat differently. First, new institutionalism in sociology, strongly influenced by economics, sees 'social institutions' in a narrower and more concrete sense as rules of conduct in social and economic transactions (Nee 1998: 1). New institutionalism studies, for example, the role of formal contracts and state regulations as well as informal codes of conduct and their enforcement mechanisms ("rules of the game" is a recurring metaphor). Second, the institutionalist framework in organization theory (also often confusingly called "new institutionalism"; see Scott 2001: 88; cf. Nee 1998: n. 1) explores the functions of institutions in organizations. Here institutions are understood as providing the setting with value assumptions, cognitive frames, rules and routines, either from within the organization or from the outside environment. In principle, this approach is rather similar to the traditional view of social institutions, but as the institutional framework is applied in the context of formal and concrete organizations, the resulting emphasis is on formal structures and legal systems, towards organized and evident institutions. Many institutional approaches to organizations are based on the assumption that organizations give form to institutions, and enable them to be studied empirically. In other words, the organization is conceived of as a kind of a container into which the institution is poured (see Scott 2001: 101).

When navigating in these different research paradigms and trying to grasp their internal disputes and contradictions, it helps to understand that we are dealing with differences of emphasis rather than completely divergent views. The picture is perhaps less confusing if we look at institutions as taking place on three different levels: abstract institutions (such as religion) give rise to more formal institutions (such as the church) that are, for practical reasons, further divided into concrete institutions (such as local parishes) with their assigned material spaces, members and recurrent activities. These levels can be viewed both diachronically and synchronically. Diachronically, one can perceive a linear process leading either towards increased formality and more concrete forms or, in other cases, from concrete systems towards a higher level of 'institutionalization'. Synchronically, these levels can be interpreted as a simultaneous hierarchy of more abstract, or 'great',[1] institutions and their more concrete and contingent realizations. In short, abstract social institutions survive and live on by being constantly reproduced in more concrete institutions.

In principle, we can study institutions on a range of levels: from the abstract level to concrete realizations, and from the world-system to the level of individuals (see Scott 2001: 87). On all these levels, institutions share a number of features: any institution can be defined as a form of uniform action governed by role expectations, norms, values and belief systems. According to C. Wright Mills (1959: 30), an institution is

> a set of roles graded in authority that have been embodied in consistent patterns of actions that have been legitimated and sanctioned by society or segments of that society; whose purpose is to carry out certain activities or prescribed needs of that society or segments of that society.

Institutions are therefore embedded in the society that endows them with legitimacy and authority. The institution endows people with particular roles, and they are then expected to act accordingly. These roles outlive their holders, thereby giving the institution consistency and stability. This consistency is a result of the normative constraints on actions. The constraints are imposed by rules, and these rules and the values and beliefs behind them all constitute an institution. While different research traditions in sociology, economics and political science emphasize different aspects of institutions, there is a shared understanding of these basic building blocks, but there is less agreement on their respective centrality.

2.2 Rules, norms and beliefs

When evaluating and categorizing the different approaches to institutions, one useful tool is W. Richard Scott's systemic view of the three pillars of

---

[1] 'Great institutions' can be seen to include language, government, the church, as well as laws and customs of property and of the family (Scott 2001: 10).

institutions. According to Scott, the three pillars – regulative systems, normative systems, and cultural cognitive systems – are all vital ingredients of institutions. They form a continuum, moving from the conscious and the legally enforced to the unconscious and the taken-for-granted. Research can either focus on one of these pillars, or view all of them as contributing to the institutional framework.

All approaches to institutions place some emphasis on the *regulative* pillar: all institutions constrain and regulate behaviour. But for new institutionalism in sociology, the regulative pillar is the focus of attention. The resulting view of institutions is: "a stable system of rules, either formal or informal, backed by surveillance and sanctioning power" (Scott 2001: 54). Compliance to rules is then coerced, and breaking them is legally or socially sanctioned.

Monitoring compliance is easier and less costly if rules are supported by norms and values. This means that the *normative* pillar can reinforce the regulative pillar. The normative pillar emphasizes normative systems, and the values behind them. Whereas values are conceptions of what is preferred and desirable, norms specify how things should be done to achieve these valued ends. Like rules, norms impose constraints on social behaviour, but norm compliance is morally governed and obliged, not coerced. In addition to the constraining factor, norms also empower and enable action by conferring rights as well as responsibilities, and they reduce uncertainty in decision making situations by providing schemata for appropriate action. The traditional institutional approach in sociology can primarily be located in the normative pillar as it emphasizes the role of shared norms and values, both those internalized and those imposed by others, as the basic stabilizing influence of society (Scott 2001: 56).

Research emphasizing the third pillar, the *cognitive-cultural* one, stresses the shared conceptions and understandings of a group. Here, compliance is based on taken-for-grantedness, routines and mimetic mechanisms, not on coercion or social expectations. Much of institutional organization theory is located in this pillar, as are the constructivist approaches to social institutions. The cognitive-cultural view of institutions stresses "the central role played by the socially mediated construction of a common framework of meaning" (Scott 2001: 58). A constructivist perspective on institutions is therefore related to process orientation. If institutions are only produced in the members' joint construction process, it is an obvious research question to ask *how* this construction process takes place (see, e.g., Czarniawska 1997). Instead of stable and rational structures, institutions begin to appear ephemeral and organic, their existence depending on the routine maintenance work provided by 'unimportant' everyday actions.

Research models with a cognitive-cultural emphasis in organization theory often lean towards ethnography and anthropology. At the same time, since the 1980s several anthropologists have turned their attention away from non-Western and primitive cultures to study 'new objects' closer at home. One central strand of this '*anthropologie du proche*' has been the examination of local, state and supranational institutions and organizations (Bellier and Wilson 2000: 2, 9). In these anthropological studies, the concept of institution refers to concrete political and/or bureaucratic organizations. The object of study can then be, for example, the institution's internal structures, organizational cultures, relations to other institutions and organizations, impact on the communities, and their role as producers of ideas and ideologies.

The three pillars represent different aspects of institutions. While there are major differences in the philosophical and ontological premises of different approaches with respect to social reality and individual agency (see Scott 2001: 61-70), it is good to keep in mind the vastness of the field that could, in principle, be covered. Each research project needs to strike a balance between the different pillars, and on the continuums both between macro and micro level analysis and between abstract and concrete definitions of institutions. While choices have to be made, and cuts need to be made, it is necessary to remember which aspects one leaves untouched. In this book, the overall ethnographic orientation adopted is best at home in the cognitive-cultural pillar. I also endeavour to include some discussion of the two other pillars, for example by studying the regulations governing translators' work and by attempting to extract value statements and normative guidelines from the official discourse (see Chapter 4). While the internal structure of the work includes the institutional macro level, the meso level of the translators, and the textual micro level, compared to studies that analyze world systems or entire organization fields, the study presented in this book is a micro-level analysis. Significantly, my choice has also been to favour a fairly concrete definition of institution. The reasons for that choice, and my definition of translating institutions and institutional translation, are discussed in the next subsection.

2.3 Institutional translation

Applying the variety of usages of the concept of institution to translation studies, on the most abstract and all-encompassing level, we could argue that the activity of translation is a social institution in itself, thus implying that *all* translation is institutional. In this perspective, all translations and all discourse about them constitute a system, or institution, of translation:

> The system of translation, as a social system, consists of all the communications processed and followed up as translational communications – and only those. The structure of the system consists of expectations about communications. The system's boundaries are constantly being

defined, affirmed and renegotiated by the system itself. (Hermans 2003: n.p.)

This kind of global view offers interesting lines of research on questions such as how translators are socialized into their profession, and how professional conduct is negotiated and monitored. In its preference for the concept of system rather than institution this view also establishes connections between the institutional approach and its closest related paradigm in translation studies, that is, descriptive translation studies (DTS) and the view of the systemic constraints of translation and translation as a norm-governed activity (Hermans 1999; Toury 1995). Adopting an analogy to sociology, the norm-based approach to translation, introduced by Gideon Toury, could be described as a control theory of translation. Toury's programmatic book, *Descriptive Translation Studies and Beyond* (1995), contains no explicit references to Talcott Parsons, or to any other social scientists for that matter, but the line of argument is similar: in every society and all historical periods, all kinds of translation activity are directed and constrained by norms, and to play the social role of translatorship within a particular cultural environment, one has to acquire the set of norms required in it (Toury 1995: 53, 57-58). Norms are not directly observable, but they can be studied by distinguishing regularities of behaviour; Toury is cautious about explicit normative formulations, because they "tend to be slanted" (ibid.: 55). On the other hand, he stresses the need to contextualize "every phenomenon, every item, every text, every act" (ibid.: 63), and normative statements are one contextualizing factor among others.

The DTS framework has proved most fruitful for historical case studies and textual analysis (shifts analysis; more recently corpus studies), but the programme Toury proposes in his book also envisions ethnographic work such as is introduced in the present study. Or at least, that is how I interpret his statement that "historical contextualization is a must not only for *diachronic* study, which nobody would contest, but also for *synchronic* studies" (ibid.: 64; emphasis in the original). The notion of norms and the idea of a system of translation are useful starting points for an institutional study of translation, but for my present purposes, the systemic understanding of the institutional underpinnings offers a framework that is too general. The concept of institutions needs to be narrowed down.

A narrower definition would argue that translation always takes place in some kind of an institutional framework. For example, Lawrence Venuti (1998) explores the marginalized role of translation in a number of institutions such as literary scholarship, the publishing industry and copyright law. This view again implies that translation is always institutional, but the understanding of institutions is different from the global approach of DTS. Venuti's approach is not dissimilar to that outlined by Brian Mossop (1990: 343):

> But translation is not simply a form of communication between individuals. When I translate a text, it is not simply me personally conveying to a reader what someone else wrote in French. It must be borne in mind that all translation takes place in an institutional context [. . .] decisions like whether to change the level of language are not made simply by looking at the genre of the text, or at who the readers of the translation will be. Rather, such decisions are to a great extent pre-determined by the goals of the institution within which the translator works.

The institutions Mossop has in mind are very different from the institutions, or systems, that provide the norms and values for the professional translation activity as a whole – and far more concrete. According to him, translating institutions include "companies, governments, newspapers, churches, literary publishers", and what he calls for is "an 'institutional' understanding of the translation process" (1990: 342). This institutional approach assumes that translators make conscious choices to adapt their translations "in the sense of making the translation serve the purpose of the translating institution" (ibid.: 345). The translators act as agents of the institution, not as individuals (ibid.: 351). In principle, my usage of 'translating institutions' is similar to the very concrete definition put forward by Mossop, but I would like to make some additional amendments. First, I do not think the translators' choices are always conscious. Second, and more importantly, while I agree that it is indeed rare to find translations that are produced outside any institutional setting (in Mossop's sense of the concept), I still argue that even within these contexts, the level and degree of 'institutionalization' differs.

Defining all translation as institutional would render a separate concept of institutional translation tautological and meaningless. In an earlier article, Mossop explicitly takes issue with the concept of institutional translation, emphasizing that his view is different:

> The translating institutions of this article are obviously concrete institutions, but not in the sense in which one often hears about "institutional translation": the translating of texts of a technical or administrative nature by large modern organizations conceived as purely economic-political entities. Translating institutions may in fact be quite small. They may produce literary translations; and in the past, they took forms unfamiliar in the modern period: a post-Renaissance patron of writers who translated is an example of a concrete institution. (Mossop 1988: 69)

Similar to Brian Mossop, André Lefevere was in favour of a concrete approach. His framework was based on systems theory, but he decidedly worked against its "forbidding level of abstraction" (Lefevere 1992: 11). Instead, his concept of patronage refers to concrete persons and institutions (such as religious bodies, political parties, publishers, the media) who have the power to further or hinder the development of literature (ibid.: 15). These patrons can execute ideological and economic constraints and grant or withhold prestige and status, and they operate by means of institutions set up to regulate literary life: academies, the educational system, critical journals, and censorship bureaus (i.e., institutions similar to those later studied by Lawrence Venuti).

As for Mossop's and Lefevere's definitions favouring concrete translating institutions, I agree. However, I believe that within these various institutions, a translation genre exists that is qualitatively different from others, and the concept of institutional translation is, I think, useful and necessary in that it captures the essence of that genre. My definition thus is as follows: we are dealing with *institutional translation* in those cases when an official body (government agency, multinational organization or a private company, etc.; also an individual person acting in an official status) uses translation as a means of 'speaking' to a particular audience. Thus, in institutional translation, the voice that is to be heard is that of the translating institution. As a result, in a constructivist sense, the institution itself gets translated. Implicitly, Mossop makes this distinction in his discussion of the readers of translations, who "construct in their mind a picture of the 'voice' that is addressing them":

> [This picture] affects the image and authority of the institution *in cases where the institution is the named author* (e.g. a manufacturer translating a user manual), *or the source-text author is identified as belonging to the institution* (e.g. a government researcher) or *the readers are aware of the institution* as they read the translation (e.g. translations appearing in newspapers). (Mossop 1990: 352; italics added)

From this definition it follows that not all translating institutions produce institutional translations, at least not all the time. Some institutions mainly rely on institutional translation, whereas some others, while perhaps actively engaged in translation, seldom do. There is, however, no clear-cut division between institutional and non-institutional kinds of translation; translations can rather be placed on a continuum or a cline of increasing institutionality. While all translations are affected by some kinds of institutional constraints, I use the concept 'institutional translation' to refer to those occupying the extreme end of the continuum. Prime examples of institutional translation would thus include: official documents of government agencies and local authorities of bilingual or multilingual countries; translations of EU or UN documents; multinational companies' consumer and stakeholder information (in cases where they are produced via translation), and so on. Conversely, a translated novel published by a publishing house (i.e., an institution) does not normally belong to the genre of institutional translation. This is because the publishing house is not the author, the novelist is not identified as a representative of the publisher, and as readers, we do not typically try to construct a picture of the publishing house voice but that of the original author addressing us via translation. Similarly, not all newspaper translations belong to this category: translated columns by foreign philosophers, for example, would fall outside this category. So, institutionality in this sense is a function of texts, not of the institutional settings *per se* (see also Drew and Heritage 1992/1998: 3). Institutionality is likewise not a function of translators, and whether the translation is produced by 'institutionalized' in-house translators or free-lancers is not a defining factor. Yet, in the contemporary world of outsourcing and subcontracting, institutional translations may well soon be the only genre where in-house translators are still employed.

My definition of institutional translation partly relies on my own translation history. Comparing my experiences as a translator of the European Commission to other forms of translation I have undertaken before and since, it strikes me as a unique case. During the fifteen years of my career as a professional translator (albeit not always full-time), I have worked in and for a number of institutional settings: I have been an in-house translator in a research institute, I have translated non-fiction and academic texts for several publishers, as well as texts to be used in government agencies, museums, schools, academic conferences and professional journals. None of these institutional settings have placed constraints on translation anywhere near as stringent as those in the European Commission. In most cases I have been given a lot of leeway, not only in the choice of words and style but often also in the overall structure and sometimes the actual content of the text. Some translations have been a result of team work, either with translator colleagues or the writers/commissioners of the translation; sometimes (especially in administrative and academic texts) it has naturally been necessary to adhere to standard terminology, etc., but essentially my translation has always been my responsibility, and consequently I have had the final say on the outcome. In all these institutional settings, my words have therefore always been mine. For me, translation has always been a personal act in the sense expressed by Andrew Chesterman (1997: 194):

> Language is individual, translation is a personal act. I myself must take responsibility for what I say and how I say it, and to whom I choose to speak. [. . .] There can be no passing the buck: the translated text is mine, with my name on (cf. Mossap [sic] 1983). I am not anonymous. It is my own trustworthiness that will either be maintained, enhanced or harmed by my translation. True, not mine alone, in that the author and the commissioner also share responsibility: ultimately we are all

accountable for this translation. And true, I may be working as one
member of a team of translators. But I alone am responsible for my contribution, and I have a loyalty also to myself. My words are mine.

Now, in the European Commission, the whole situation is quite different.
There language is not individual but quite heavily controlled, and translation
is not a personal act but a collective process, where I as an individual translator can only assume a limited responsibility for what I say, to whom and how.
The translated text is not mine, nor does it have my name on it: it belongs
to the institution, and it bears the name of the institution on it. It is not my
trustworthiness but the trustworthiness of the translating institution that will
be maintained, enhanced or harmed by my translation. In the Commission,
my words are not mine; I am a spokesperson for the institution. The institution speaks through me.

This intuitive feeling that institutional translation is in some ways different
from other translation genres, and that adopting a different kind of orientation
is required from the translator so as to produce institutional translations was
at first a very pragmatic problem for me. As a newly recruited translator, I
found myself in unknown territory that I needed to understand and come to
terms with. I also realized that I needed to develop a new kind of professional
identity to fit my new institutional role. This initial confusion was also the
catalyst of the research project that forms the basis of this book. However,
pinpointing the causes for these intuitions is not that simple:

> Although it is easy enough, on an intuitive basis, to identify a variety of
> ways in which activities seem to be done "differently" in institutional
> settings, it is much more difficult to specify these differences precisely
> and to demonstrate their underlying institutional moorings. (Drew and
> Heritage 1992/1998: 20-21)

I have found it useful to see institutional translation as a form of auto-
translation.[2] Organizations (indeed, officially seen as legal persons) can be
seen as personified super-persons: they "learn, unlearn, produce strategies, and
do all the things individuals usually do" (Czarniawska 1997: 41). Although
of course this is just a metaphor, and, as Czarniawska argues, represents an
objectified and monolithic picture of the reality, it is also telling. Besides the
many other 'individual' things institutions do, they also produce documents
and translate them. Significantly, in institutional translation, the institution
is typically the author of both the source text and its translation(s). Thus,
institutional translation is self-translation.

---

[2] I am grateful to Chantal Gagnon for bringing to my attention this viewpoint and Hermans'
paper (2003).

In literary contexts, when authors self-translate their own work, the translated text is not considered less authentic or secondary. Instead it is rather seen as being an equally valid expression of the same authorial intention in another language. In institutional translation it is often important, symbolically or for practical purposes, to maintain that the different versions of a particular document are equally authentic and equivalent. The communicative function (or *skopos*) of the source text and its translation is a constant: although the different language versions are targeted to different sub-groups of the audience, the 'authorial intention' in them remains the same (Šarčević 1997: 21). Hence the need for maintaining the 'illusion' or 'legal fiction' that multilingual legislation is simultaneously drafted in several languages (Koskinen 2000a). As Theo Hermans (2003) points out, these texts may well be translations in a genetic sense, but they no longer function as such, and in this sense 'authenticated' translations are similar to self-translations or autotranslations.

To produce the image that the institution speaks to you directly in many tongues, the translator's role needs to be effaced. Institutional translation therefore often (although not always) hides its translational origins (for example, the European Commission does not produce 'translations' but 'language versions'). As a consequence, the individual translator is but an instrument of multilingualism. An awareness of this position is also clearly evident in my focus group data, in the translators' descriptions of their role within the commission. One participant explained, "I'd say we have instrumental value". "We do not have any substance value, unfortunately". Another one continued: "We are a necessary evil to the Commission".

My usage of the term 'institutional' is, to an extent, analogous to its usage in conversation analysis (CA), a method of detailed analysis of talk-in-interaction, which is often applied in 'institutional' contexts. Paul Drew and John Heritage, who first coined the term 'institutional talk', delineate their object of study as those interactions where "at least one participant represents a formal organization of some kind" (1992/1998: 3). A famous dictum by John Heritage claims that institutions are "talked into being". It could be further claimed that in multilingual settings institutions are to a large extent translated and interpreted into being, and similar to institutional interaction, institutional translations represent a formal organization of some kind. But, knowing how slippery the concept of institution is, what is meant by 'institutional' in CA? Answering this question is complicated by an explicit aim of many representatives of this approach to leave the central concept of institution open-ended. Drew and Heritage explicitly deny the possibility of hard and fast distinctions between institutional and ordinary talk and refuse to offer a definition, or even attempt a synoptic description (ibid.: 21). Similarly, the editors of a casebook of methods for analyzing institutional talk announce that they "take the term 'institutional' loosely" and that the term is "not intended to carry important analytic or theoretical weight" (McHoul and Rapley 2001: xi). This strategy of ducking the issue may be handy, but it is not very helpful in analysis.

In the absence of either analytic definitions or synoptic descriptions, the relevant meanings have to be construed from individual arguments. Synthesizing the main claims made by Drew and Heritage, one can maintain that: (1) institutional interactions are task-related, (2) they involve at least one participant who represents a formal organization of some kind, (3) participants' institutional or professional identities are somehow made relevant to the work activity, (4) the participants' conduct is shaped or constrained by their orientations to social institutions either as their representatives or 'clients', and (5) institutional interactions are **not** ordinary conversation (Drew and Heritage 1992/1998: 3-5).

Conversation analysis uses 'ordinary talk' as a kind of benchmark against which institutional types of interaction are measured and compared. It thus has to take the difference between the two as a given and postulate institutional talk as an out-of-the-ordinary phenomenon (see Drew and Heritage 1992/1998: 19). Institutional talk is work-related (not casual); it involves issues of professional identity, and assumes that at least one of the participants represents either a formal organization or a social institution. Keeping in mind the very different definitions of social institutions in traditional sociology and new institutionalism, the first option, formal organization, seems to be more useful. Considering the way in which CA distinguishes between institutional and ordinary conversations, the notion of social institutions is problematic. For example, many sociologists would define family as a social institution *par excellence*, but in the CA categorization, family discussions are not interpreted as being institutional (Drew and Heritage 1992/1998: 59; cf. Hester and Francis 2001: 208-210). In any case, emphasis on formal organization is closer to my definition of institutional translation: translation is institutional if the translation represents a formal organization of some kind, if the translation in fact translates the institution itself. To sum up, and to make the *double entendre* of this book's title explicit, I argue that institutional translation means *translating the institution*, not just providing translations for a translating institution.

2.4 Categories of translated institutions

Language is an important element in the bureaucratic institutions of today: the daily work of most employees largely consists of writing memos, drafting documents and policy papers, reading reports and discussing them in meetings. In addition to the internal text work within and between institutions, the external relations to different constituencies are also text-driven in the form of PR material and guidebooks, instructions and directives, application forms and personal letters. Conversely, in contemporary societies we citizens can hardly avoid these text-based contacts. In pre-modern societies, most people lived their lives without more than sporadic contact with institutions such as armies, state bureaucracies and church organizations. In contrast, the life of most people today is shaped by regular interaction with institutions: as employees of state organizations or big companies, and as clients and consumers of various public services. For this reason, institutional language use in its various forms is both a central feature of institutional work and a significant element of our daily life (Czarniawska-Joerges 1992: 1).

Multilingual institutions complicate the issue further: in the EU context, for example, the linguistic and semantic features currently need to be multiplied by 23 (following the accession of Bulgaria and Romania, and the inclusion of Irish), and there is no likelihood that any document is either delivered or received in an identical manner in all these languages. The role of multiple languages and translation is, however, seldom brought to the forefront in anthropological, or political, studies of the European Union. The central role of discourse practices, and the consequent necessity of studying official discourses and languages, is often acknowledged (e.g., Bellier and Wilson 2000: 8). Some projects do focus on institutional discourses. For example, Gilbert Weiss and Ruth Wodak have conducted an ethnographic and linguistic analysis of the discourses and decision-making processes in the European Union, where they observed the work of an advisory committee of the European Commission and focused on the genesis of a policy paper in that group's discussions (Weiss and Wodak 2000). The analysis of shifts of meaning and rhetorical devices (cf. Chapter 6) reveals how aspects such as business-speak and globalization rhetoric dominate the procedure. It is nonetheless curious how monolingual the drafting process represented in Weiss and Wodak's article appears to be. The only hint of more than one language (English) being involved is one transcribed example of a comment made in French. Issues of translation remain outside the focus of interest. Owing to the centrality of translation in the discursive practices of multilingual institutions, an obvious need has arisen for more input from translation studies. Considering the amount of translation work in the EU institutions and its widening geographic and linguistic reach to present and future candidate countries, it is surprising how little research on EU translation has been carried out in translation studies.

Translating institutions (that is, institutions commissioning translations) are not a unified set of organizational contexts. Similarly, *translated* institutions (that is, institutions that get translated in and by institutional translations) are numerous. Some of these institutions are large, international conglomerates while others are small, local units; some employ a veritable army of translators (the European Commission has some 1,750 in-house translators, and the figures are rising), others employ just a few (the small bilingual municipalities in Finland, for example, may employ only one or two translators), and yet others rely solely on outsourced translations. While the basic tenets of institutional translation are not dependent on the size, location or prestige of the institution, issues of power, status and authority colour the contexts in numerous and significant ways. The various settings for institutional translation are regulated differently by legislation and official requirements (the regulative pillar). Institutions also differ in their approaches to institutional translation, and the related customs and (usually unwritten) guidelines are in no way uniform (Šarčević 1997: 22) (the normative pillar). It follows that the underlying rationale for institutional translation can result in a whole range of different translation strategies and routines, and different translation cultures and professional roles can emerge (the cultural-cognitive pillar). Understanding institutional translation thus requires 'local explanation', that is, detailed case studies of different institutional contexts. The latter part of this book focuses on a supra-national institution, the European Commission. However, it is useful to contextualize the Commission not only among supra-national institutions, but also by contrasting it to institutional translation in other kinds of contexts, closer to the everyday life of people. For clarity, I have divided institutional translation into three categories, different not only in size and language combinations but also in their social role and position. The categories are: supra-national institutions, multilingual and bilingual national administration, and public services.

Supra-national institutions

It has been argued that we are living in an age of complex organizations (Czarniawska-Joerges 1992: 2). There are a number of reasons for the proliferation of large organizations. Besides an increased national bureaucracy and a tendency towards chains and mergers in the business world, it is clearly evident that the age of globalization has also been an age of supra-national institutions: in 1909, there were 37 inter-governmental organizations and 176 international nongovernmental organizations (NGOs) in the world; by 1989 there were approximately 300 inter-governmental organizations and 4,200 NGOs (Cronin 2003: 109). Organizations such as the United Nations, the European Union, the International Monetary Fund, the World Trade Organization, NATO and the Council of Europe, together with their surrounding international NGOs, all represent the twentieth-century movement "away from an exclusive concentration on the sovereign nation-state toward models of political and economic governance which are deterritorialised in nature" (ibid.). Most of these international organizations are based on foundational multilingualism and a set of working languages (the UN has six, the IMF and NATO have two, and the ambitious EU programme now has 23).[3] It follows that these international organizations are also based on foundational translation and interpretation. During the past fifty years, there has thus been an explosive growth in the volume of institutional translation, since these supra-national and multilingual institutions are largely discursive and information-intensive by nature:

> [T]he vast majority of international organizations are heavily dependent on information both to inform *and* to give effect to their decisions. Any decisions which are taken that lead to the signing of international agreements and/or to the incorporation of appropriate measures into national law require the preliminary information-intensive activities of meetings, conferences, discussion documents, reports, media handling and so on. In addition, information in the form of data on the operations and decisions of the organizations must be provided to members, and as these supra-national entities function in a multilingual world of increasing complexity, they must perforce manage projects and activities across many different languages and cultures. (Cronin 2003: 110)

At the same time, global markets have made it necessary for business corporations to go international, either by building a supranational organization structure, or by aligning themselves with international partners. In their internal communication, global business organizations are to a large extent able to choose their preferred company language, thereby eliminating their need for company translation services but also transferring the actual translation processes to the shoulders of individual employees whose native language is different from the company language. Language policies are, however, also officially regulated. For example, companies functioning in several European countries are expected to organize joint meetings with their employees for consultation and information (European Works Councils), and the directive (95/94/EC) tacitly assumes the availability of interpretation in these events. External information is also regulated by consumer rights, since products need to be accompanied by adequate documentation – the more and more globalized business world thus advances the buzzing localization industry (i.e., translation by a new name).

Multilingual and bilingual administration

The often massive quantity of translation and interpretation in supranational institutions, both in the number of languages included and in the texts and

---

[3] The language policy of the European Union institutions is often seen by critics as being an excessively costly and foolhardy attempt at superficial equality. Another view is expressed by Michael Cronin (2003: 111), who notes that the European Union may prefigure emerging post-national political entities and the related specific translation challenges.

events involved, makes them a prime example of institutional translation. But the central argument of this book is that translation work in these organizations is not qualitatively different from other institutional contexts perhaps involving a lesser number of languages and confined within one national context. In countries with more than one official language, multilingual administration and legislation is a central locus of institutional translation. A large bulk of translation work is routine, but the political and sometimes highly sensitive nature of language policies and the related power relations often add tensions. Regionally based linguistic divisions with clearly remarketed borders seem prone to creating antagonistic situations (Quebec; Flanders vs. Vallonia), but bilingual administration can also be rather uneventful and tensionless. For example in Finland, where the official use of Swedish is not limited to a particular geographic area but varies municipality by municipality based on the size of the Swedish-speaking minority (or, in some municipalities, the Finnish-speaking minority),[4] there is remarkably little drama or public debate concerning this issue.

In countries such as Canada, Belgium and Finland, bilingualism has a long history, and language relations are more or less stabilized. The postcolonial era has also propelled massive new projects of institutional translation as ex-colonial states shift their administrative language policies or as previously monolingual administrations turn multilingual. One such case is the Republic of South Africa, which, since 1996, has operated in eleven official languages plus a number of acknowledged minority and 'heritage' languages (see Dollerup 2001). Another recent example is Macau, where the relative positions of the Portuguese of the previous colonial rule and the Cantonese of the present government have changed, and translation relations have changed accordingly. Language issues are very much in the forefront in postcolonial countries, and the newly acquired independence and the new official role of indigenous languages needs to be balanced with the role of the language of the previous power holders, be it English, Portuguese, Russian, or any other language. In politically sensitive contexts, language policies and their spin-offs in terms of translation and interpretation are unavoidably politicized. Much as translators

---

[4] In addition to the two national languages, Finnish and Swedish, there are two minority languages in Finland: Sámi (a regional minority language used in Lapland), and sign language. According to the Sámi Language Act, the Sámi have the right to use either Finnish or Sámi before the courts of law as well as before the state and municipal authorities whose jurisdictional or administrative areas cover all or part of the Sámi Homeland. The authorities in that area are obliged to use Sámi in their written communication with individuals and when disseminating information to the general public. Sign language is officially acknowledged as a mother tongue for the deaf, who have the right to 120 hours of free sign language interpretation per year (in the context of education, the hours are not limited). Additionally, the islands of Åland form an autonomous, Swedish-only, region.

may wish to remain impartial, they are engaged in power play through their work. This is always the case in institutional translation; turbulent times just make the engagement more visible, because the shifting power nexus makes it necessary to recalibrate translation relationships (Cronin 2003: 156).

Public services

Power relations and differences in the status of different linguistic groups have a role to play in defining the context of institutional translation in its various forms. Most countries have specific stipulations designed to ensure that official languages are adequately catered for in the daily functioning of public services: pupils are taught, expectant mothers are given advice, speeding tickets are written, marriage vows taken and estate inventories made in any official language, limited resources allowing (cf. Dollerup 2001). For immigrants and minorities without official status, the story is quite different. Obviously there are no resources to cover the multitude of languages, nor would it make much sense to attempt to provide such cover. It is, however, worth noting that even in small and remote corners of the world such as Finland, we are currently witnessing an unprecedented flow of immigrants, and dealing with their different languages and cultural backgrounds is becoming a daily experience for many working in the public services. Furthermore, there is no reason to expect the tide to turn; quite the contrary: "If it is predicted that over 80 per cent of the world's population will be living in cities by the end of this century, and migratory flows are unlikely to cease, then Babel will be on our doorstep, everywhere" (Cronin 2003: 170-171).

In contrast to the organized and legislated framework of institutional translation in both supra-national organizations and multilingual administration, institutional translation and interpretation in public services is often based on ad hoc solutions, volunteer work and language brokering. While interpreting and translating services in Finland are legally provided for in (certain) official contacts with institutions, in most daily situations the speakers of minority languages are left to their own devices. Of the two, community interpreting is better organized and resourced, and also researched within interpreting studies. For official contacts with, for instance, immigration and school authorities, the police and the health care system, community interpreting is available in several, although not all, minority languages spoken in Finland (in Finland, some 120 languages are spoken; 60 languages are available for community interpreting). 'Community translation' on the other hand is less visible, although in practice this work is also carried out in community interpreting centres, and the official guidelines stipulate that information material should be provided in minority languages. To reduce the Babelian confusion of languages, in Finland it has sometimes been suggested that to enhance our competitiveness, we should assign English an official role that would define the range of administrative documents and legislation to be translated into this global *lingua franca* (cf. Phillipson 2003). Another strategy, recently employed in the Social Insurance Institution of Finland, is to make the documents written in Finnish as plain and accessible as possible so that even those with limited linguistic abilities can understand them. In addition to immigrants and minority language speakers, this strategy in fact helps *all* readers, and as a long-term strategy, it reduces translation and interpretation needs.

In some countries, the cohabitation of a national language and several community languages has a long tradition, and the relative status of each language is established. Compared with such multicultural metropolises as London or New York, the situation in Finland is completely different. First, the main national language, Finnish, is hardly spoken outside Finland, and it is not feasible to expect immigrants to have a good – or, in fact, any – command of it upon arrival. Second, Babel arrived at the Finnish doorstep only recently: in spite of the existence of some indigenous minority languages in Finland (in addition to Swedish, Sámi, and sign language, which are recognized minority languages, Romani and Russian have long traditions in Finland), the flow of new languages is a recent phenomenon. In 2003, there were 107,100 foreigners living in Finland. Compared to the figures in many other countries, this is a very small fraction of the population. Nevertheless, the scene is rapidly changing, and Finland is becoming more and more multicultural. In ten years, the foreign population has doubled (55,600 in 1993) (source: Population Register Centre; see also Leinonen 2001). Third, the groups of speakers of each language are relatively small, and there are no 'chinatowns' in Finnish cities: speakers of minority languages cannot live isolated from other languages. Serving immigrant and refugee clients – and having them as colleagues – is a new experience for many Finns, and coping with language problems is likewise a new challenge.

In public services and in administration in Finland, Finnish is the dominant language, and often the source language of translation. For example, in legislation, the Swedish versions are nearly always translated from Finnish. In the context of supra-national institutions, the situation is different. There, Finnish is among the small, lesser-used languages, and typically assumes the role of target language. For example, in the European Commission, English and French are the two source languages, all the others being mainly target languages (Lönnroth 2005). In spite of the differences in power relations, all these instances of institutional translation attest to a changing and enhanced role of the Finnish language (from a geographically limited language to enjoying an official supra-national status) and to the on-going change of Finland from a relatively monocultural (although bilingual) and isolated community to an increasingly multicultural member of a supra-national alliance.

2.5 Translating institutions and translator training in Finland

The needs of institutional translation tend to be reflected in translator training. Countries with a long tradition of bilingual administration also tend to have established translator training programmes, providing for the steady demand for translators between the official languages (see, e.g., Mossop 2006). In Finland, Swedish is traditionally catered for in translator training, whereas Sámi is not included in the curricula of any translator training institute. The main languages of the European Union are taken into account, although this is more a coincidence than a question of conscious planning: since it began in the 1960s, translator training has been available mainly in English, German, Swedish, Russian and French, but the field was not quite prepared for the sudden increase in demand for French translators and (even more so) interpreters in and around 1995 when Finland joined the EU (see also Pym 2000: 12). Today, the European Union institutions are involved in the training of interpreters in tailor-made interpreter courses at the Universities of Turku and Helsinki. For the EU, this institutional involvement is a sensible move:

> After all, if good professionals are hard to find, it is logical to create an elitist *esprit de corps*, to set in place the conditions for the future training of professionals, and to take steps to counter the proliferation of poorly trained sub-professionals. The EU has had to create a professional caste of interpreters, and it needs to ensure appropriate conditions for the controlled reproduction of that caste. (Pym 2000: 13)

As Pym (2000: 13-14) continues, from the point of view of the training institutions, risks are involved: there is no reason to believe that the ideologies and linguistic needs of the EU institutions are the ones that best serve the society as a whole and are to be used as a model for interpreting or translation practices outside that institutional context. The European Commission has recently also taken a more active role in shaping translator training across Europe. Its proposal for a 'European Master's in Translation', promoted by the European Commission[5] (e.g., Lönnroth 2005), however, does not appear too detached from traditional translator training programmes, nor is it explicitly geared towards the needs of the European institutions.

A powerful institution such as the EU is better placed to 'force the hand' of training institutions, or even to set up its own programmes if deemed necessary. To fulfil the needs of the less resourced institutions and less prestigious

---

[5] For the proposed curriculum, see http://ec.europa.eu/dgs/translation/external_relations/universities/master_curriculum_en.pdf.

languages, little training is available. Of all the 120 foreign languages needed in the public services in Finland (in addition to the major European languages), university-level translator training is only available in Russian. Russian was not originally included in the programmes to address the needs of community interpretation and translation for the largest group of foreigners in contemporary Finland;[6] the explanation for its inclusion since the very beginning of translator training is rather to be found in the strong commercial ties Finland has traditionally had with Russia (or, in particular, the former Soviet Union).

As Michael Cronin has pointed out, "it is worth considering whether translation schools and scholars should look not only to the languages within countries but also to the languages without" (2003: 170). In Finland, the traditional translation schools have been slow to adopt a new perspective on the distribution of languages. Instead, there have been separate initiatives to provide training for sign language and community interpreting. Different from the traditional translator education, these courses and programmes are not offered at the MA level: sign language interpreters are trained in polytechnics, and community interpreters in immigrant languages often have no formal training at all or have participated in a short-term vocational training course (Leinonen 2001). The lower and less established education also results in less income, attesting to the status differences between languages and language users.

Differences in volume, legal status and relative power and prestige in different institutional contexts make the field complex. Translating is not a restricted profession, and practising translators have different educational backgrounds. Established training courses only cover a fraction of the languages. The role of translators and interpreters in different institutional settings is also different: the in-house translators of the European Commission are in many ways tied to the institution they speak for; community interpreters are professionally and administratively detached from both parties (but the regional interpretation centres are established and resourced by the Finnish government...) and are to remain impartial. Between these extremes is a multitude of different institutional settings and a spectrum of institutional practices for coping with multilingualism.

---

[6] The total number of Russian speakers in Finland at the end of 2003 was 35,222, of whom 24,988 were Russian nationals (National minorities in Finland, http://virtual.finland.fi/net-comm/news. Accessed 21.12.2004).

3. Ethnographic Approach to Institutional Translation

3.1 How to research institutional translation?

An institutional approach emphasizes the situated nature of translation and brings several aspects to the forefront that constrain and regulate translators' work. On the basis of the three pillars of institutions, as constructed by Scott (see Chapter 2 above), an institutional analysis can focus on (1) the rules and regulations governing institutional translation practice, (2) the norms and values constraining and guiding translators' actions, and (3) the shared conceptions and understandings of the translators. All these contribute to the institutional role(s) accorded to and assumed by the translators. Understanding institutional translation, in this case in the EU context, thus seems to revolve around the questions of how the translators see their institutional role and what they are expected to do.

In an article on EU translation, Anthony Pym (2000: 16) lists a number of key questions in need of answers. Many of them are directly related to the translators' institutional role and professional identity: "Do EU translators work in the name of their languages and cultures, or is there an EU intercul-ture? When the crunch comes, which way do professionals decide?", "Is the professional vision of translators inward toward the intercultural institutions, or outward toward receivers who are not in intercultural positions?" Some of the questions are related to the texts: "To what extent do translation strategies influence the public perception of the EU?", "Do EU translators have the power to add to or to take away from the texts they work on?".

These questions are among those this book addresses and seeks to answer. But how can those answers be found? Analyzing translation as an institutional practice forces the researcher to reconsider which methods and what kinds of data might best illuminate the institutionality of institutional translation. Two aspects seem essential: first, translation is a textual activity, and to understand it one needs to examine the (source and target) texts produced within the insti-tution in question. Second, 'institution' is a sociological concept, and taking the institutional context into account directs the research towards questions related to social action. An institutional approach therefore needs to combine the study of texts and the study of people and human interaction. This ap-proach needs to situate both translations and translators within the institutional context. Yet how do we distil the institutional features of texts? How do we collect reliable data on peoples' actions and attitudes? And how do we relate and connect the findings of the two?

This is where ethnography, with its combination of both attending to detail and aiming at a holistic interpretation, can be of assistance. Ethnography, the "Swiss knife" of research (Sulkunen 2003), allows for complexity in research design: it uses multiple sources of data (basically anything – any artefact, any piece of conversation, any text fragment – can be used as data) and analyzes them through multiple methods. In fact, any method can be made to work for an ethnographic analysis. Furthermore, ethnography is not confined to one single setting (multilocal, transnational and virtual ethnographies are quite fashionable at the moment) or a single time frame (cyclical processes; collective and individual memories). It can therefore accommodate both the study of translations, the study of translators and the study of the institutional context where they work.

Ethnography is first of all a methodological choice, offering a robust and adaptable framework for a situated analysis of a particular group of people or a cultural locale. However, that choice also has larger ramifications beyond the practical issues of selecting data and methods of analysis. Ethnography can only be practised in an intimate relationship with the object of study. This intimacy – at least as compared to more detached modes of, say, text analysis or archive research – pushes to the forefront the personal and ethical aspects of the endeavour. Consequently, issues such as the researcher's identity and the informants' degree of privacy become more acute. The aim of this chapter is thus two-fold. First, it offers a short introduction to ethnography in general and in studying translation. Second, it includes a discussion of the philosophical and ethical underpinnings of ethnography.

3.2 Essentials of ethnography

Traditional anthropology and ethnographic work were originally related to studying foreign and exotic tribes (e.g. Malinowski 1922; Levi-Strauss 1955). Even so, there is another long tradition of ethnography 'at home' in sociology. Its roots can be traced to the work of a group pf scholars referred to as the Chicago School in the 1920s-1930s. An often cited seminal work is William F. Whyte's study *Street Corner Society* (1943), based on his long-term fieldwork among the street gangs of 'Cornerville', a Boston slum. More recently, fields such as education, health, social policy, media and market research have applied ethnography as a research method (Atkinson and Hammerslay 1994). In the UK, linguistic ethnography has recently gained in popularity, uniting researchers interested in combining ethnographic methods and linguistic objects of study. In these applied fields, fieldwork is often condensed, and the focus narrower than in traditional ethnographies. The most important difference, however, is in how ethnography is perceived: the focus in these applied fields is not on anthropological theories of culture and cultural interpretations but on using ethnography as a methodology to solve practical problems. The ethnographic approach applied here is akin to these latter ones. I use ethnography as a method for contextualizing EU translation and for understanding the cultural context in which EU translators work. Regardless of the aims and goals of research, there are in ethnographic work some fundamental values and principles also cherished by these 'applied' and 'focused' ethnographies (see, e.g., Hammersley and Atkinson 1983; Schwartzman 1993; Silverman 2001: 43-78). The ones most central for this study include the following:

- Ethnography is a holistic study of a particular culture, or community, and the aim is to attend to both the everyday details and routine text production as well as to the wider social context. It searches for answers to questions such as: "What does it mean to be a member of this group?"; "How are these texts produced?"; "What kinds of cultural artefacts are these texts?"
- Ethnography is based on multiple methods and diverse forms of data, and the enquiry is open-ended and theoretically emergent. That is, this approach is not based on testing a prior hypothesis or pre-developed theory but disposed to taking new turns as findings accumulate. However, I do not approach my subject as a *tabula rasa*, without any pre-existing conceptions (no-one ever does), but from the practical viewpoint and theoretical understanding gained from an earlier position as an insider within the same field I have later approached as a researcher.
- Ethnography requires engagement with the object of study – going into the field – and a willingness to learn from those who inhabit the culture.
- The researcher's role is central: *my* observations, *my* interpretations, *my* knowledge and understanding, as well as *my* personal contacts and *my* skill in eliciting information (and *my* limits in all these) delineate the research. In an important manner, ethnography is a "hauntingly personal" enterprise (Van Maanen 1988: ix). This inbuilt subjectivity also calls for extensive reflexivity. My own position is that of a 'marginal native' – once an insider, now an outsider.
- Moral responsibility towards the group under study is highlighted: formal consent and permission do not diminish the requirement to be sensitive to the extent one can or should in terms of exposing and exploiting others' personal experiences.

There is no one correct way of doing ethnography, and there is no unified understanding of it across anthropology, sociology, theology, organization studies, work place studies as well as across the numerous other disciplines where ethnographic methods have been increasingly employed during the past few decades. As such, ethnography is not a 'technique' that can be mastered. Rather, ethnographic orientation as it is understood here provides a loose methodological framework and ethos for the research process. The researcher's ethnographic stance entails a commitment to an open-ended research process; it aims at understanding a social phenomenon by making sense of it through engaged observation and interpretation. Ethnography aims to be a dialogic combination of different viewpoints, those of the observer and those of the observed, and a combination of different kinds of data, those elicited or provoked and those occurring naturally. *Ethno*graphy is an attempt to understand the way of life of a particular folk group, and, significantly, ethno*graphy* is a textual process. Ethnographic fieldwork is followed by 'deskwork' as the dialogic encounters and findings are woven together by the researcher to build up a tale from the field (van Maanen 1988; see also Atkinson 1990).

3.3 Ethnography in translating institutions

Ethnographic methods are not commonly used in translation studies, but there has recently been growing interest in related approaches. Several researchers have pointed out the affinities between translation/interpretation and anthropology (Sturge 1997, 2007; Wolf 2002; Bahadir 2004). There are also indications of a new practice-orientation and new empiricism in translation studies, giving rise to engaged observation methods and practical fieldwork. Practical ethnographic research on translation is rare, but its relevance may be growing in importance. Sociologists are talking about a new 'practice turn' following the linguistic turn in the social sciences (Alasuutari 2006: 87); the emerging sociological trend in translation studies may indicate a similar shift of emphasis. In recent and on-going projects, researchers have been encaged in fieldwork in translation agencies (Risku 2004), among subcontracting translators (Abdallah, forthcoming), in publishing houses (Buzelin 2005), as well as in interpreted conference sessions (Diriker 2004) and authentic community interpreting situations (Leinonen, forthcoming).

   Empirical work that is based on ethnography and fieldwork methods could in fact perform a strategic function in translation studies, not dissimilar to the role of ethnography in sociology. According to Sharrock and Hughes (2001), ethnography can help sociology overcome its methodological problems of relating abstractions to actualities and of bridging theory and research. One can easily discern a similar use in translation studies, with its perhaps undue traditional emphasis on general theories. Recently, these general theories – such as systems theory and skopos theory – have given way to more data-driven approaches. For example, corpus studies have made a significant contribution to translation studies by providing new kinds of *quantitative* data on the linguistic aspects of translations. Ethnographic approaches can similarly enrich the field and support theory-building by providing methods for eliciting new kinds of *qualitative* data on the social aspects of translation. Ethnography could also give methodological support to descriptive translation studies and cultural approaches to translation. In other words, ethnography is not to be seen as a radical new departure but rather as a new set of tools to analyze the contexts of translation.

There is a long tradition of using ethnography in organization research and in linguistic studies of work-related 'discourse communities'.[1] The extensive literature on ethnographic work in organizational settings provides ample support for similar endeavours in translating institutions. Since interpretation is more easily 'observable' than translation, the social aspects of interpreting have received more attention. The tradition of 'practisearchers' in interpreting studies (a concept coined by Daniel Gile to describe practitioners interested in theorizing; cited in Pöchhacker 2000: 80) may also have contributed to the growing emphasis on practice-orientedness in interpreting studies, whereas translation studies may have been more prone to 'armchair theorizing' (Holmes, cited in Pöchhacker 2000). Studies focusing on translation could therefore benefit from experiences gained in interpreting studies, where participant observation and other fieldwork methods of data collection (with or without an explicit ethnographic framework) have been applied (for an overview, see Pöchhacker 2004: 151-152 *et passim.*; see also Gile 1998). Ethnography could also be used as a theoretical umbrella for joint projects simultaneously analyzing and contrasting both translating and interpreting practices of a particular site (European Union institutions and various community interpreting/translating services, for example, would offer excellent cases), thus bridging the unnecessarily wide gap currently dividing research on the spoken and written modes of language mediation.

Institutional translation is well suited for ethnographic analysis for a very practical reason: reliance on in-house translation implies that in most cases, translators are physically gathered in translation units where they can be observed. To appreciate the difference this makes, one can compare the project coordinators Hanna Risku (2004) studied with the translators the company employs: the coordinators are all sitting in one room; the more than one thousand freelance translators affiliated with the company are dispersed in various different countries around the world. In her study, Risku focused on the coordinators; subcontracted translators located all over the world were not explicitly included in it. For an aspiring fieldworker, their virtual community would be a far more challenging site – but also a fascinating object of study!

---

[1] For an overview of organizational studies, see Martin (2002) and Schwartzman (1993); for examples of linguistic (genre) analysis with an ethnographic perspective, see, e.g., Swales (1998); Candlin and Hyland (1999).

Risku is interested in exploring how the workers observed accomplish their *work-related tasks*; she is less committed to finding out about their world views, attitudes, or loyalties. This focus is similar to the one found in the model proposed by Mossop (2000). While my research design shares affinities with many workplace studies, it follows the basic tenet of traditional anthropology in that the present study aims at producing a cultural analysis. There is no doubt that workplace procedures in the translation units of the European Commission would provide fascinating objects of study, or that the technological environment so central to the translators' work would yield important new information on the interaction of humans and computers or on the actual uses of translators' tools. However, these aspects are subordinate in this study to a more holistic approach: it is my aim to attain a deeper understanding of the professional identities and cultural affiliations of the translators in the Finnish translation unit, to understand how they see their tasks and responsibilities, how they fit in and contribute to the overall drafting process, and where their loyalties lie. To accomplish this aim, a short observation and interview period alone is of limited value. After all, culture cannot be grasped during a short visit. For this reason it was essential that I myself had earlier been a member of that cultural scene.

3.4 Probing cultural relations

Operationalizing culture

Ethnography, the study of cultures, always implies a theory of culture, but what the concept of culture actually means has become a tricky issue. This concept has become overused and under-defined across the humanities, and the 'culture worry' experienced in anthropology (see Silverman S. 2002) is shared in many disciplines: there is little agreement on exactly what is meant by culture, and much uneasiness, apprehension or defensiveness around the different usages. In organizational studies, the debates have been sufficiently vehement to be described as "culture wars" (Martin J. 2002: 29). Culture is a tricky concept, and its different usages can easily result in mutual misunderstanding. I will not dwell on the issue here.[2] Instead, I will try to make explicit how culture is understood in this study, and in particular, how this concept has been operationalized for research. Amongst the various understandings of organizational culture, I have found the view expressed by Joanne Martin (2002: 1) most useful for my purposes and highly compatible with my world view. I quote it at length:

---

[2] See, e.g., Schein (1991); Martin J. (2002); Fox and Kling (2002). For a discussion of the concept of culture in translation studies, see Koskinen (2004).

When organizations are examined from a cultural viewpoint, attention is drawn to aspects of organizational life that historically have often been ignored or understudied, such as the stories people tell to new-comers to explain "how things are done around here", the ways in which offices are arranged and personal items are or are not displayed, jokes people tell, the working atmosphere (hushed and luxurious or dirty and noisy), the relations among people (affectionate in some areas of an office and obviously angry and perhaps competitive in another place), and so on. Cultural observers also often attend to aspects of working life that other researchers study, such as the organization's official policies, the amounts of money different employees earn, reporting relationships, and so on. A cultural observer is interested in the surfaces of these cultural manifestations because details can be informative, but he or she also seeks an in-depth understanding of the patterns of meaning that link these manifestations together, sometimes in harmony, sometimes in bitter conflicts between groups, and sometimes in webs of ambiguity, paradox, and contradiction.

Significantly, Martin's definition does not even attempt to specify what culture 'is' but rather more practically aims at describing where cultural aspects are *manifested* and *observable*. This approach provides a tightly packed research agenda that merits a closer analysis. First, it tacitly assumes that organizations can and should be studied from a cultural viewpoint, and it brings to the forefront the subject doing the studying, the 'cultural observer'. Martin's claim of ignored and understudied aspects, here, refers to perceived gaps in organizational studies, but if we want to apply this to translation studies, the claim is even more acutely true. What is to be studied then are stories, anecdotes and jokes, the physical environment and atmosphere, relations among people, official policies and formal arrangements, and so on. The objects of study are, to put it succinctly, both material and ideational.

The aim of Martin's approach is to achieve an in-depth understanding of the surface manifestations, but there is no *a priori* assumption that all cultural aspects are shared by all members of the community; the patterns of meaning can be harmonious, conflicting or ambiguous. It is, Martin (2002: 108) argues, largely a question of emphasis and world view, whether a researcher decides to concentrate on aspects that are shared (the integration perspective), on subgroup differences and conflicting interpretations and the power relations behind them (the differentiation perspective), or on irresolvable ambiguities and inner contradictions (the fragmentation perspective). Martin's own definition entails paying attention to all three of these.

Applying Martin's definition to the case of EU translation, and relating it to the three pillars of institutions discussed in chapter 2 above, we also notice that it entails aspects of all three pillars. The regulative pillar includes such issues as official policies and translators' terms of employment. The normative pillar consists of the norms of translation and the unwritten norms of acceptable behaviour and attitude. Finally, the socio-cultural pillar encompasses issues such as the stories and jokes the translators make of themselves and others, sarcasm and laughter as ways of dealing with ambiguous situations, and the physical work-place settings. In an ethnographic approach, all these are analyzed from a cultural viewpoint, in an effort to link them so as to obtain an in-depth understanding of the patterns of meaning behind these manifestations. The aim is, to rewrite Clifford Geertz's famous punch line, "to figure out what the devil [the translators] think they are up to" (cited in Martin J. 2002: 37).

Some manifestations are easy to observe: some documents deal with official policies, and the physical space is visible for any visitor. But it is more difficult and time-consuming to observe attitudes and behaviour related to translation. Compared to occupations such as those of interpreters and project coordinators, whose work is largely talk-based and interactive, observing translators who are busy at work yields little naturally occurring data to help figure out what exactly they think they are up to. Since cultural affiliations are not necessarily among the primary issues of explicit debates (unless there is an acute crises or the researcher probes the issue), coffee break discussions and informal gatherings may offer limited opportunities to elicit explicitly stated information (although observing manifestations such as seating arrangements and topics of discussion can also be valuable). Unless the researcher wants to set up an experiment based for example on think-aloud protocols, a method rather removed from the general ethos of ethnography, the most obvious way to generate more data is simply to ask the translators themselves. Ethnographers often use individual thematic interviews, but one can also opt for group discussions or focus groups to elicit focused data. These group situations offer an opportunity to both collectively interview the participants as well as to observe their interaction during the discussion. For some issues, such as my focus on professional identity, interaction in focus groups can be particularly productive (for a similar case, see Suter 2000). This is because focus groups can provide valuable information on both accepted attitudes and contested views, both shared experiences and unique perspectives. Furthermore, by relating these discussions to other kinds of data, a researcher can discern potential tensions and problem areas and map the limits of acceptability (for more on focus groups, see Chapter 5).

Interviews and group discussions elicit qualitative data; their input can be complemented by quantifiable methods and statistical data gathered from official records or collected by administering surveys or questionnaires. Viewing (organizational) culture as something manifested and observable opens up further possibilities for gathering quantifiable data on aspects such as terms of employment, employees' housing arrangements, annual newspaper subscriptions, TV channels or lunchtime companions. These data can be used as indications of professional relations and cultural affiliations. In the research project reported in the following chapters, I administered a questionnaire to gather information on these and related issues (see Appendix 2).

Nexus approach to culture

I have argued elsewhere (Koskinen 2000a and 2000b) that EU institutions pro-duce translations out of, or within, a multinational EU culture. In other words, translations are either *intra*cultural or *inter*cultural. Intracultural communica-tion takes place within one institution or between them (intra-institutionally or inter-institutionally); intercultural communication reaches beyond this EU culture to the various constituencies located in the national cultures. My view of translators as mediators between the EU culture and their own national culture has its roots in how I perceived my own task as a translator, but this view is also largely compatible with the conclusions of an anthropological study on the Commission. An internal anthropological survey (Abélès *et al.* 1993: 6) maintains explicitly that the Commission has a culture of its own, consisting of an ensemble of shared values and notions which create a feeling of a common identity. This identity, however, is complex and multilayered (*'feuilletage d'identités'*), since the civil servants identify not only with the Commission but also with their particular directorate, with their nationality or their homeland.

This view of EU institutions having formed a culture (or separate cultures for different institutions) of their own has met with some criticism. For ex-ample, María Calzada Pérez, who tested my notion of intercultural translation on her data consisting of speeches delivered and translated at the European Parliament (EP), found no evidence of a particular EU culture (Calzada Pérez 2001; see also Koskinen 2004). On the other hand, Anthony Pym has put forward the hypothesis of intercultural spaces, that is, places located on cul-tural intersections and inhabited by various intermediaries such as diplomats, traders or spies (Pym 1998: 188). This would entail that the EU institutions form not a culture but an *inter*culture. "Translators", argues Pym, "have at least hovered around intercultural communities. To say much more, we would need to know more" (1998: 189).

These disagreements and different conceptualizations suggest that it may be sensible to undertake a more in-depth analysis of the translators' cultural af-filiations. These differences can be rationally explained by different viewpoints (my insider experience versus Calzada Pérez's outsider analysis) or different concepts (my EU culture need not be different from Pym's interculture; we have just chosen different name tags), but they suggest there is indeed a need to know more. For this reason it makes sense to focus on the issue of cultural affiliation, and to study EU translation and EU translators from the perspective of culture. A focus on the translators' organizational culture can also offer new insights into organizational science where 'border jobs' (professions engaged in inter-organizational and intercultural mediation) have been identified as a challenging new area for researchers of organizational culture (Martin J. 2002: 323).

The theoretical starting point of this study is that wherever there are people, there are manifestations of culture (which can be placed under scrutiny). But since cultures are not isolated islands, the borders between cultures are always constructions, and drawing them is often a process open to criticism from all sides. I will therefore leave the issue of EU cultures or intercultures pending, and approach the question using a more open-ended strategy. For the purposes of this study, I will view culture as a relational concept, accepting the permeability of cultural boundaries. Instead of positing an institutional EU culture and seeking to find evidence of shared beliefs, symbols, values, and attitudes (i.e., an integrationist perspective), I will adopt a 'nexus approach'. This means that the translation unit is conceptualized as a nexus in which a variety of internal and external influences come together (see Martin J. 2002: 162-164). I will view the unit as a contact point of various relations from within the Commission, from other EU institutions and outside them. These different relations are the threads I use to weave the net around the translators.

The nexus approach is predominantly fragmentational in that it anticipates conflicting interests and ambiguous positions. This undoubtedly has a bearing on the results: it is unlikely that an analysis geared towards ambiguity would result in a clearly defined picture of the object of study – in all likelihood it will present a fragmented view. Thus it is not likely that a nexus approach will result in a picture of a uniform EU culture, but I hope the open-ended approach will advance our knowledge of the cultural affiliations of the translators working in and for institutions, whether we choose to call those institutional contexts 'cultures', 'intercultures' or something else.

3.5 Identifications

Split identities

One could argue that everything human is also cultural, that "culture implies all aspects of human life" (Schein 1991: 246). For a researcher interested in studying a particular culture, this is both good and bad news: the research area is practically infinite. This gives the researcher a great deal of leeway in designing the project (herein lies the source of many conceptual skirmishes and debates over the best research practice), but it also follows that each approach is unavoidably partial. The nature of ethnographic research adds to the problem: data collection can in principle go on for ever, and the researcher just needs to make a decision as to where to stop. Similarly, in a natural setting, there are always several synchronous events taking place, and the researcher can only be in one place at one time. The researcher cannot observe everything, nor focus on all manifestations of a culture with similar intensity. As a result, choices need to be made.

The nexus approach to culture emphasizes cultural *relations*. The related concepts of (organizational) culture and (organizational) identity can be defined in terms of embeddedness: identity is the culturally embedded understanding of oneself in relation to the larger system (Fiol *et al.* 1998). These relations are placed under closer scrutiny in Chapter 5, where the focus is on manifestations of identification and disidentification, on how to find answers to the identity questions (who am I?/who are we?) by negotiating the degrees of affinity in various relations. Manifestations of identifications can be sought from a number of perspectives, including the role of laughter, humour and sarcasm, the points of agreement and disagreement between the participants, the unsaid (the limits of group discussions), indications of cultural affiliation or lack of it, the points of defensiveness, the ingroup/outgroup categorizations, and, finally, from stories and anecdotes.

Opting for the concept of 'identification' rather than 'identity' is a conscious choice. Identity (similar to 'culture' and 'institution') is notoriously difficult to define, and I also deliberately wish to refrain from claiming that my research could somehow reveal the true, and monolithic, 'identity' of translators. Instead, I aim to locate what kinds of identifications can be discerned. This focus on identification is merely one way of approaching culture; it can be used as a lens through which one can observe cultural life. Previous work in translation studies suggests that a relational approach might be a fruitful starting point. Ever since Friedrich Schleiermacher, many discussions have portrayed the translator amidst conflicting interests, debating whether to bring the writer to the reader or the reader to the writer. Translators, because of their profession, are caught in the middle: between the source text and the target text, between the reader and the writer. Their loyalties are (to be) split (Nord 1991). This bilateral commitment is often seen to put translators in the role of negotiators and mediators, leaving little room for their own personal feelings of affinity or distance. Translators are responsible for safeguarding the rights of all parties. It follows that loyalty is largely a cognitive concept: translators are to watch out and rationally balance the situation. But how does this system of split loyalties function in practice, and how do people cope with conflicting demands in their everyday work? Or do translators, in fact, experience the split or conflict at all? We have little empirical information on this, and my focus on identification aims at adding to this knowledge.

Another related discussion is centred on the notion of love. The rhetoric of gender, sexuality and the different forms of fondness has a long history in the discourses on translation:

> Thus theories of translation have been peopled, metaphorically, with chaste maidens, mistresses and unfaithful lovers. Translators have worried that the process of translation may violate the purity of the mother tongue, and that bastards would be bred. Translators have worried equally over the virility of the original, and the complaint is frequently that the original has been emasculated. The act of translating has been compared to sex, and to rape. (Chamberlain 1998: 94)

Texts and their writers can be sheltered from the horrors of infidelity, bastards, and emasculation when translators are expected to love and honour their sources. There was an interesting revival/reversal of this discourse (Chamberlain, curiously, does not mention it) within feminist translation in the 1990s: the traditional notions of fidelity were criticized and replaced by new, openly sexual metaphors advocating "mutually pleasurable orgasmic encounters" (Susan Bassnett, as cited in Arrojo's critical overview of feminist theories, 1995) and experiments outside "the habitual 'missionary' position assigned to translation" (von Flotow 1991: 82). I have personally found it difficult to accommodate the idea of love into either my theoretical thinking of translation or my work as a translator. In the context of identification, the rhetoric of love, however, has a valuable contribution to make: it takes into account the emotional side of interaction. After all, identification is not just a question of rational choice; as humans, we also bring in our beliefs, feelings and needs. A comprehensive view of identification needs to encompass the "thinking, feeling and acting person" (Harquail 1998: 223).

Both the notion of loyalty and the notion of love posit that translators are in a position where their loyalties need to be controlled. A different view is offered in Anthony Pym's notion of specific intercultures, where the translators are detached from any national affiliations, and their loyalty is expected to be directed towards the intercultural space and to enhancing intercultural communication (1997). Theoretical discussions thus provide a fertile soil for investigating translators' affiliations and loyalties. For example, are the translators impartial negotiators between the communicating parties or are they loyal to one or the other group? Are they emotionally engaged in their work (do they 'love' the source texts/their readers/the writers)? Do they mainly identify with the other inhabitants of the intercultural space of the EU institutions, or are they rather 'hovering around' the intercultural EU community? And since they are not only thinking and feeling but also acting, is there a correlation between their words and deeds?

In exploring the institutional identity of a clearly defined professional group, my aim is not to unravel individual identities but to try and understand how they function as a group. I am not examining the identity of the individual translators but the social identity of a particular occupational group – that of the Finnish translation unit. Social identity theory supports the presupposition that social categories serve as a system of orientation in that individuals use their group memberships in the construction of their self-identities. This happens because groups produce categorizations by making comparisons with other groups and by clarifying ingroup/outgroup boundaries (us/them). An element of self-enhancement is involved here; intergroup comparisons tend to be favourable to a person's own group. One can thus explore the social identity of a group by analyzing the categorizations that emerge in discussion: which groups are seen as being similar, and which as different? Furthermore, who are considered to be out and who in?

Questioning identification

The multilingual and multinational context of the EU institutions brings to the fore issues of identity – both within the institutions and in their relations to the constituencies outside the institutional discourse community. These institutions are challenging workplaces, forcing people to rethink their identities:

> For those people who work in EU institutions, converting a national being into a European one, jumping into a multicultural if not Babelian world, is not as simple as might be suggested by the word 'Eurocrat', which is often used pejoratively to refer to the agents of the European Commission and other EU institutions. The European Commission is the 'laboratory' where officials, recruited from all the member states, commit themselves to serve 'Europe', thus taking a position on the future which might affect their perception of their national identity. (Bellier and Wilson 2000: 17)

For translators, the professional group whose explicit task is to bridge the gap between the insiders and the outsiders, the issue of identification is even more pressing and perhaps also even more complex than for other officials. There are several possible directions of affiliation and identification at EU translators' disposal: for example, the EU institutions in general (or 'Europe'); the other civil servants of the Commission; other Commission translators; (Finnish) EU translators in other institutions; translators in general; the Finnish readers of their translations; or their adopted new homeland (see Chapter 5 and Appendix 1).

In examining the translators' nets of relations, it is necessary to include in one way or another the issues related to their personal life and families. It has been argued that, since organizational policies affect the well-being of the families of employees and vice versa, a study of organizational culture is incomplete if it does not take into consideration the individual's personal life and family members (Martin J. 2002: 325). This is particularly true in the case of EU translation: upon accepting the post, the translator is required to move abroad, and whether the family chooses to travel along or stay behind, the employment has fundamental effects on the whole family. Anthony Pym (1998) has emphasized the need to view translators as human beings with material bodies and material needs. His point, central to his notion of inter-cultures, is that translators *can* move (outside their point of origin). Within the context of EU translation, they not only can but *must* move. Most of the Commission translators (although not all) take their families with them, and the Commission amply supports this. But there always remain ties to their earlier homeland in the form of friends, relatives, memories and material belongings. And since the translators' task is to reach out to this same point of origin with their translations (most readers of Finnish translations are located in Finland), their professional and private ties are closely knit.

Issues of cultural relations and identification are at play in all kinds of settings for translation, but they are highlighted in institutional translation. In Chapter 2, I defined institutional translation as covering those cases when an official body uses translation as a means of 'speaking' to a particular audience. This means that in institutional translation, the voice that is to be heard is that of the translating institution – not that of any individual writer, nor that of the translator. This creates a particular emotional twist: if you are to give a voice to an institution in your daily work, to speak on behalf of it, issues of identi-fication become more pressing. Whether you support the same causes as the institution or personally disagree with the messages you participate in sending, or whether you elaborate a conscious detached indifference, the question of identification is more in the forefront than in some other kinds of translation. Membership in an in-house translation unit (that often goes hand in hand with institutional translation) functions in the same way: a freelance translator may find it easier to disidentify (or impossible to identify) with an institution when an occasional translation job is the only connection with it. In public services, the translators and interpreters are often themselves immigrants, and may identify more with the newcomer in need of linguistic assistance than with the institution paying for the service. A tenured in-house translator whose spouse is covered by the organization's health care and insurance system and whose children go to the international school set up specifically for them has many more reasons to feel strongly about the organization. Institutional translation thus begs the question of identification.

Textual identities

The notion of identification also pertains to the documents in all their language versions. This interpersonal aspect of EU translation was delightfully brought to the forefront in an internal Commission seminar in April 1999, where I introduced the first draft of my taxonomy of EU translation, divided into intrainstitutional, interinstitutional and public documents (see also Koskinen 2000a): the categories were translated by the participating Commission translators as corresponding to 'family', 'friends' and 'foreigners'. These personalized categories emphasize the varying degrees of closeness: when communicating within the circle of our family members or close friends, we can use strategies that are strikingly different from those used when communicating with total strangers. The extent of shared knowledge and pre-existing social ties lubricate the flow of communication between intimately familiar communicating partners.

Similar to translators' discussions, the Commission documents can be interpreted from the point of view of identifications and cultural relations. An analysis of categorizations and identifications within the texts can offer important insights into institutional discourse. EU documents are not known for their accessibility, and they are often criticized in the Member States. Analyzing the textual ingroup/outgroup construction can help us understand the problematic reception history of these EU documents. The institutions of the European Union have been built to fulfil particular tasks. In order to accomplish their tasks, the institutions produce agreements, legislation, policy papers, reports, rulings and decisions, and so on. That is, they produce texts. All these pieces of text are simultaneously instances of discursive practice (of text production and interpretation) as well as instances of social practice (Fairclough 1992: 4). While the explicit tasks of the institutions do not include creating and monitoring cultures and identities, in practice that is precisely what these texts are actively trying to do: building the European Union is fundamentally a legitimation process, and the institutions must get the support and approval of the people, who in turn need to be remodelled into "European citizens" (Bellier and Wilson 2000: 15, 21). This support has not always been easy to secure for the institutions. It has been argued that in addition to a democratic deficit, a 'cultural deficit' also exists, that is, a lack of fit between the citizens and the 'European' elite cultures (Wilson 2000: 137). Since the encounters between the EU 'elite' and its various constituencies are typically text-mediated rather than personal, it makes sense to look for the reasons for the perceived cultural deficit in the discursive practices found in written documents.

The internal workings of these institutions are often based on spoken discourse as well – meetings are held, issues are discussed. In external communication, written texts dominate. The European Parliament is, to an extent, an exception, but in fact the speeches delivered in the parliament live on as written documents: the MEPs "speak for the minutes of the session" (Abélès 2000: 41). Only a handful of spokespersons speak on behalf of the institutions, but the institutions issue a steady flow of written documents designed for various audiences. The institutions produce texts, and the texts produce the institutions. Since the external communication of the European Union institutions is largely text-based, their corporate identity and the degree of positive identification by the citizens largely depend on how successful the written documents are in creating the desired effects. Furthermore, since the European Commission is a translating institution, external communication is also predominantly translation-based, and translators thus in practice exercise extensive ideological and discoursal power, although this power is not reflected in their status (see Fairclough 1995: 41).

EU texts are not famous for their interpersonal and emotional power. On the contrary, in public discourse these texts are often considered bureaucratic, technical, repetitive, or legislative, and seldom seen as instruments for building attachments or creating personal relations. But interpersonal aspects are always present in communication, and all communication can be studied from this perspective. In systemic-functional linguistics it is assumed that texts have three simultaneous metafunctions: ideational, interpersonal and textual (Halliday 1985: 53). The ideational function pertains to the representation of experience and the world; the interpersonal function constitutes social interaction between the participants; and the textual function ties the parts of a text into a coherent whole (Fairclough 1995: 6). The analysis of the case document in Chapter 6 addresses the interpersonal function. This analysis aims to uncover how the institution creates and maintains interaction with its various partners, and how it posits itself and others in the text.[3]

A number of textual features can be related to the linguistic construction of interpersonal relations. In addition to explicit linguistic resources such as address or naming, interpersonal relations can be maneuvered, for example, via modal verbs, lexical choices (specialized language/slang/everyday words), judgements and appraisals, or polarization and thematization (Martin J. R. 1997: 21). Lack of a particular linguistic feature can also be indicative of interpersonal relations: both a bald and blunt command and a softened and

---

[3] To what extent, then, is it accurate to claim that institutions talk, or engage in auto-translation? Or, are institutional discourse practices but a collection of the individual representatives' haphazard choices? The metaphor often used by genre theorists can be helpful: institutions provide the rules of the game, and individual actors need to learn how to play by the rules – and also how and when to bend them (Bhatia 1999). Institutional genres function as a stabilizing framework, orienting both writers and readers towards standardized formulas and interpretations, but they are not a mechanical determination system: rules can be ignored, patterns can be changed.

interpersonalized request indicate particular relations of authority (Iedema 1997). It is not incidental that these features are similar to those listed by Drew and Heritage (see 1992/1998: 29-53) as resources through which speakers "evoke and orient to the institutional context of their talk". In the institutional conversations studied by conversation analysts, the speakers orient to a particular interpersonal relation: that between a representative of an institution and an outsider (layman/patient/client). In addition to the resources directly related to spoken conversations (such as turn-taking, sequence organization, or overlap/interruption and topic change), institutional talk is characterized by features such as lexical choice (technical vocabulary indicating specialist knowledge and institutional identity), the use of *we* (speaking on behalf of the institution), cautious expressions (neutrality), and the use of task-related standard patterns. Additionally, institutional interactions are characteristically asymmetrical in their distribution of knowledge and access to participation. These features, identified in spoken discourse, can also be studied in the context of *written* institutional discourse.

3.6 Who is who: Positioning myself

Reminiscences

Fieldwork is at the heart of ethnography. The ethnographer attempts to acquire a comprehensive understanding of what is going on in a particular pocket of society, and seeks answers by entering the scene and trying to make sense of it. The ethnographer is thus positioned *in* the field, and can adopt a number of different roles. The often used fourfold typology of complete observer, observer as participant, participant as observer and complete participant (Atkinson and Hammersley 1994: 248) is merely a shorthand for the endless variations and possibilities that can take place during the different phases of a research project. But whatever role the researcher is able and willing to choose, that choice affects the outcomes of research.

Owing to the nature of ethnography, the researcher's personality is a central research instrument. The deeply personal aspects of fieldwork largely revolve around issues of identity. As a result, during the fieldwork I conducted for this analysis, I found myself asking again and again not only who the translators I am studying are but also who I am – and who would I have been had I not chosen the academic path. The first question, the identity of the translators, is the one I consciously set about to investigate, but the more personal questions have unavoidably arisen in the process of this undertaking. In an important way, fieldwork is identity work where the identities of both the observer and the observed get reconstructed:

> The construction and production of self and identity occurs both dur-
> ing and after fieldwork. In writing, remembering and representing our
> fieldwork experiences we are involved in processes of self presentation
> and identity construction. In considering and exploring the intimate
> relations between the field, significant others and the private self we are
> able to understand the processes of fieldwork as practical, intellectual
> and emotional accomplishments. (Coffey 1999: 1)

Contrary to a view of innocent and ignorant ethnographers entering the scene of research with no previous assumptions about it, ethnographies of occupational settings are often produced (e.g., in nursing and education) by members or ex-members of the setting who are already knowledgeable and empathetic (Coffey 1999: 33). This competency often facilitates entry and helps in gaining acceptance, but it also propels the researcher into roles and processes that are not always comfortable. Re-entering the field of EU transla-tion made the memory of my earlier experiences as one of the translators more vivid, and the observation and interview period was not only a research trip to gather data but also – to an extent I had not anticipated – a trip to the land of 'might-have-been'. Interviewing my former colleagues and analyzing their life style and work setting, I found myself also engaged in pondering who *I* would have been had I chosen to stay. This underlying question did indeed also affect my research agenda: my emphasis on issues of identity and cultural affiliation and the less central role I accorded to workplace arrangements may, with hindsight, be a result of my personal history. As I was already familiar with the organization of work, it did not intrigue me, whereas the question of professional identity remained a mystery to me throughout my short career and afterwards. It made sense theoretically to ask the question of culture, but it also made sense personally.

While reflecting on the decisive choices affecting my life history is, naturally, of extreme relevance to myself, it is of little interest to the reader hoping to be enlightened about institutional translation. But an awareness of my background is relevant for interpreting the analysis I offer below since, in the sense of using myself as a research instrument, I have tried to employ my identity work strategically to benefit the analysis. That is, in reading and rereading my notes, transcriptions and documents, I have consciously tried both to identify with the translators, imagining the hypothetical 'I who stayed', and equally consciously at other times to distance myself and assume the role of an outside observer.

One way of taking advantage of previous personal experience is to actively engage in retrospection and reminiscence, and to treat one's memories as an additional set of data. It has been argued that ethnography always is "an act of collective and individual memories" (Coffey 1999: 110). This is even more relevant for ex-members who need to adjust their own experiences to the new (and potentially changed) reality they encounter as researchers. In cases such as mine, the success of the short observation period was completely dependent on the earlier (field)work of 'observant participation'. Blurring the division between participant and observer violates a basic rule of classic anthropology: the assumption that the researcher can penetrate into the alien society and gain a thorough understanding of it, but at the same time retain her critical distance and objectivity. The paradoxical nature of this calling is expressed by anthropologist Ruth Behar (1996: 5) as follows:

> Our intellectual mission is deeply paradoxical: get the "native point of view," *pero por favor* without actually "going native." Our methodology, defined by the oxymoron "participant observation," is split at the root: act as a participant, but don't forget to keep your eyes open. [. . .] [W]hen your grant money runs out, or the summer vacation is over, please stand up, dust yourself off, go to your desk, and write down what you saw and heard.

Since the late 1980s, anthropology and the study of organizational culture have been going through an 'identity crisis'. Like many other fields in the humanities, the critical, feminist and postmodern tendencies have questioned the earlier paradigms.[4] There has been growing dissatisfaction with the earlier 'realist' and objective rhetoric, and increasing anxiety over the aims and place of the discipline in (post)modern academia. Behar's solution to the paradox of engagement and non-commitment has been to advocate an extremely emotional and personal way of writing, 'vulnerable anthropology that breaks your heart'. The claim of unobtainable objectivity is countered by turning to extreme subjectivity. In the extreme, this view would embrace a solipsist world view, assuming a fundamental inability of anyone to understand the life of anyone else – an *impasse* for any ethnographic endeavour. There are also potential exhibitionist traits in bringing the researcher's person to the forefront (not to mention the possible embarrassment of boring the reader with uninteresting details of personal history…), and extensive self-reflection can easily be interpreted as self-indulgent and arrogant, or a form of intellectual lethargy (Pym 1998: 30).

These doubts aside, Behar's vulnerable ethnography is an important reminder of the researcher's unavoidable presence, both during the research process and in the written end product. It is not my aim to engage in autobiographical writing, nor do I think there is an emotionally moving tale to be told about my

---

[4] A similar development has taken place in translation studies in the 1990s (see Koskinen 2000b). On postmodernity and reflexivity in ethnography, see Marcus (1994).

stay in the Commission, but my personal history is entangled with this research project to a greater extent than in my previous research. As a consequence, I have needed to rethink both my roles and engagements and the driving forces and motivations of my research agenda, and it seems only fair that the reader should be made aware of my position. So to conclude, whereas the thrust and motivation of this work is away from my personal experience and towards a more general account of translation work in the Commission, during the project it became obvious to me that the personal cannot be dispensed with. Inevitably, my quest for increased objectivity has resulted in an increased understanding of the eternal return of the personal. I have thus included personal accounts when they have had a bearing on my analysis or argumentation to enable the reader to assess their weight methodologically – or to judge for themselves the extent of my bias.

Since my previous visit to the *Jean Monnet* building in 1999, world events had brought new security measures applied to all visitors. One new development was that in addition to a paper form to be signed by the inviting official, everyone visiting the building was expected to wear a visitor's badge visible at all times. Leaving my passport at the reception and putting on the badge every morning during my stay was a constant reminder of my true status. I was no longer a participant; I was just visiting. The same is true of my former unit: although I felt I was a welcome visitor, it was obvious that my researcher role affected the interactions. I was accepted, and my queries were tolerated, but only up to a point. I was allowed to see a glimpse of their world, but it would be foolish of me to believe, or to let the reader believe, that I am still an insider of that world. On the other hand, I am not a complete outsider either. This dilemma of being located on the border, one foot inside, the other outside, is easily discernible in the transcribed discussions I had with the translators. In an effort to build a confidential and trusting atmosphere, I repeatedly refer in the discussions to how things were when I was there, and rush to make clear that I know the whereabouts of things in the building and am familiar with in-house slang words (such as "fisu" for *fiche de travail*). It is fairly obvious that my unconscious aim was to 'pose' as one of the gang (cf. Coffey 1999: 28-31). But, of course, I was not. Not quite.

The problem of the degree of insiderness in this kind of 'halfie research' of occupational settings is similar to that of 'native anthropology', that is, anthropology as practised by those who have a personal connection to the community they are now studying. To what extent can you call yourself a native of, say, a rural village in the Caribbean Islands, if you have been living in a major US city for the past twenty years or so? How native do you need to be to pass as a native? And if you go too native, will you lose your observer stance and critical perspective? Will your native insights enhance or hinder your analysis? Do they make it more or less reliable?

In translation studies it is quite common for researchers to have previous or simultaneous experience as translators or interpreters. There are even cases of scholars analyzing their own translations (see e.g., Venuti 1995). We do not, however, have many explicit discussions of the complexities involved in this kind of dual role. It seems that we are not accustomed to translation scholars inscribing their personal history in their analytic writing.[5] Ethnographic approaches can advance discussions and awareness of researcher positions not only in fieldwork but also in other kinds of inquiry. But they also highlight the difficulties entailed. In ethnography, there is a traditional division between *emic* and *etic* perspectives, that is, between adopting the informant's viewpoint and seeing the field from an outside perspective. The division becomes untenable if the dividing line is located inside you. The line between the participant and the observer, insider and outsider, friend and stranger, becomes difficult if not impossible to draw. In such a case, the continuing ambiguity that colours the entire research process has to be somehow acknowledged and made visible in reporting as well. This ambiguity cannot be held back in the hope of acquiring an aura of increased objectivity, but it can be productively used to benefit the analysis. Joanne Martin (2002: 328) points out that a marginalized or deviant person who moves to the edge of culture can be crucially important for the research project because he or she defines what is 'in' by being 'out' or 'almost out'. If it is the researcher who is in this marginalized role, tapping the personal emotions and feelings can enhance the analysis. Nevertheless, this process requires a self-reflexive analysis of one's position, and this position also needs to be made transparent to the reader.

Ethical considerations

Ethnography aims to penetrate, describe and interpret another person's life. Any self-reflexive analysis of the role of the researcher thus needs to confront questions of ethical responsibility and power: to what extent do I as a researcher have the right to expose the life choices or inner feelings of those who kindly shared their experiences with me? There are limits of intimacy that one needs to be sensitive to and that are not to be crossed in research reports. Basic rules such as informed consent, written agreements or the right to preview the text before publication only set the formal framework; they do not absolve the analyst of moral responsibility.

In many ethnographies, this problem of intimacy has been alleviated by 'anonymizing' the site and the informants with the help of pseudonyms. This course of action has limited viability in the case of the European Commission:

---

[5] A notable exception is Anthony Pym (e.g., 1997; 1998) who often builds his theoretical argumentation on his personal background.

if the study includes an analysis of the documents, their EU origin is close to impossible to camouflage, and the language versions can be pinpointed to particular translation units. The emphasis of locality in ethnography further makes it difficult to hide the geographic location of the unit. For this reason it seemed rather futile to try and hide the fact that my research focuses on the Finnish translation unit of the European Commission in Luxembourg. But beyond that, anonymity has been maintained to a certain extent, as follows: the individual translators who were observed and who took part in the focus group discussions are sheltered by anonymity, and I have tried to avoid including comments, discussions or details of personal history by which individual translators could be identified in the published report, even though this may sometimes weaken the argumentation. In these instances, moral responsibility towards the people involved perforce overrides academic responsibilities.

However, there is no escaping the position of power that goes hand in hand with the researcher role. Much as ethnographers can emphasize the ethical treatment of the informants, portraying themselves as 'marginal natives' or posing as one of the participants, the ethnographer controls the research and writing process. This is because the representation offered to the readers is based on the researcher's choice of what is important and how it should be interpreted. This dominant position is more obviously visible in anthropologies of native tribes with no command of Western languages. In contrast, our contemporary informants, like those interviewed and observed in this study, are quite capable of speaking for themselves and able to control and contest the researcher's views. Similarly, the choice of inscribing myself in the text is an attempt to counterbalance a power structure in which I as the researcher use my position to define my object of study, i.e. other people's identities. Even so, the basic hierarchical structure remains: in ethnographic projects it is the researcher and not the informants who designs the research process, decides on its thematic focus and writes the report. In academic fields of publication, the author needs an academic position to speak from in order to command an audience.

Other questions that need to be considered from a moral perspective are related to the longer-term effects of the project. The researcher has to reflect on who benefits, or suffers, from the research. For instance, will my results help advance the aims of the European Union? Or is it rather a critical intervention that offers people tools to understand – and be less vulnerable to – the ways in which the EU attempts to convey its message? Or both – or neither? Another question pertains to whether this study has some repercussions in the life of the informants, and if so, are they for better or for worse? Finally, whichever way these questions are answered, can I accept the consequences? These issues are always present in research, but ethnography brings them to the forefront. This approach does not easily allow the researcher to take a position of a neutral describer but forces one to think through one's own motives and objectives. In doing so, this method relates to a more general trend in various approaches to translation studies to develop ways of critical intervention into the practice of translation (on critical translation studies, see Koskinen 2004).

It would be foolish to expect that one academic study, however insightful, can have fundamental social effects, but neither should we be blind to the political and ideological underpinnings of all research, however neutral and objective it purports to be. Ethnography has traditionally been directed towards contributing to academic knowledge rather than towards solving practical problems. As the use of ethnographic methods has spread to different disciplines, more practice-oriented than traditional anthropology, there has been a change of ethos, and applied forms of ethnography have taken a different stance on carrying out research specifically designed to address a particular practical problem, sometimes in commercial applications (Atkinson and Hammersley 1994: 253). This study has not been funded by the Commission, nor has it been directed by its needs; it is also not my intention to 'speak for the natives', as they are quite capable of speaking for themselves. The main thrust of my work is academic: this is an invitation or a call for action in the sense that I feel that a dire need exists in translation studies for extended empirical work. However, I am not denying that I also hope that I will be able to contribute to the improvement of translation practices and processes in the European Commission and to making the role of translation more visible both inside and outside the Commission. Nevertheless, it is a sobering thought that "the impact of fieldwork is usually greatest for us and not for our hosts" (Coffey 1999: 37). This research project has most certainly had a more lasting impact on me than it will ever have on either translation studies or on the translation unit. It has forced me to rethink not only my research practices and my researcher identity, but also my career path and life choices.

Part II

Translation in the European Commission

4. Language Work in the European Commission

4.1 Institutional ethnography

In the introduction to her study of the EU administration, Anne Stevens (2001: xix) posits a number of questions related to the role and identity of the civil servants working in the EU institutions:

> Who are the Brussels bureaucrats, how much influence do they have over the outcome, and to whom are they accountable? How do they relate to one another and to national and local administrations within the complex network of EU institutions? Do they have an agenda of their own, and if so do they have the power and influence to carry it forward? Where do they come from, and what sort of ethos, administrative and cultural traditions do they bring with them? Is a collective European administrative culture emerging, and if so what is it like?

The task I have set myself is rather similar to the one Stevens sets out to investigate, but limited to the subgroup of translators. The questions I ask concern who the Commission translators are, and where they are located in the complex network of relations? Do they have an agenda, and do they have power? What are their cultural affiliations? In this second part of the book, answers to these kinds of questions are sought by means of three different routes. The next three chapters add different kinds of threads to the net I am weaving around my case, that is, the Finnish in-house translators working for the European Commission in Luxembourg. First, I will explore the institutional setting where the translators are located (this chapter). The 'institutional setting' is to be understood here both in an abstract sense, referring to the norms and regulations governing the role and status of the translators, and in a very concrete sense, referring to the physical environment and material conditions of their workplace. Second, the translators themselves are given the floor, and an analysis is presented of their group discussions concerning issues related to questions of status and identity, and of their answers to the questionnaire concerning their cultural affiliations (Chapter 5). Third, the role of translation/translators is studied by conducting a close analysis of a translated text, searching for indications of how institutional processes and practices are inscribed within the text, and how the texts in turn construct the identity of the institution (Chapter 6).

Reality, of course, is not divided into separate sectors or chapters. The structure of my presentation is thus a forced simplification of a complex network of factors. For the sake of clarity, I have mainly kept the three levels with their different data and methods in their separate chapters, but in some cases it has been more informative to blur the divisions and put the different findings in direct dialogue. My method is to weave one thread at a time. In the closing chapter I try to pull all the threads together.

According to Gubrium and Holstein (2001: 16), institutional ethnographies "combine an ethnographic eye for the scenic influences of institutional life with a discourse-analytic ear for situated talk and interaction". This description covers the two first levels of my analysis: first, the institutional setting and, second, the discourses the translators employ when they construct their tasks and roles in a group setting. The special nature of this particular professional group adds a third dimension to my institutional ethnography: an analysis of the textual products the Commission translators participate in drafting.

This chapter focuses on the institutional and physical setting and is mainly based on two sets of data. First, it relies on an analysis of official institutional documents which frame and regulate translation work; second, it is based on the results of the observations I made during my visit. The core documents include: Council regulation No 1 (1958), the Staff Regulations of Officials of the European Communities (http://europa.eu.int/comm/dgs/personnel_admin-istration/statut/tocen100.pdf), White Paper on European Governance (COM (2001) 428), report on European governance (2003-2004) (SEC (2004) 1153) (staff working document), Action plan to improve communicating Europe by the Commission (SEC (2005) 985) and selected parts of the web pages of the European Union institutions (www.europa.eu.int). The analysis of these source documents is thematically focused: my reading is limited to issues pertaining to the problems at hand and I only discuss those aspects which have a bearing on translation and translators.

The ethnographic observations are mainly based on my visit to the Finnish translation unit in June 2004. These findings are mixed with the memories of my own previous experiences. Although this second set of data is qualitatively different from the documents, its function is similar. I read both the documents and the material settings from the point of view of locating the spaces occupied by translators, and use these administrative and physical locations as keys to understanding their role and place in the institutional system. That is, I engaged in a practice of 'researching from a particular location', taking the translators as the nexus of my analysis and reading all my data from their perspective (Campbell 2003).

4.2 Framework documents

Institutional multilingualism

Multilingualism is fundamental to the European Union. The very first council regulation (1958) stipulated the official languages (then four, now, after succes-sive enlargements, twenty-three) and established the citizens' right to address the EU institutions in any of the official languages and to receive an answer in that same language. The principle of the multiple authenticity of the documents and the requirement that the institutions both speak and listen to all official languages was later further reinforced in the EC treaty (see Wagner et al. 2000). An official web brochure rationalizes the language policy as follows:

> The reasons why the European Union needs 20 official languages are not hard to find: they are democracy, transparency and the right to know. EU legislation applies throughout the EU, and therefore to all its citizens. New legislation must be published and made available to them in their own language. As in any democracy, each citizen has a fundamental right to know why a particular item of legislation is being adopted and what it requires him or her to do. It is also a basic tenet of the European Union that all its citizens and their elected representatives must have the same right of access to the EU and be able to communicate with its institutions and authorities in their national language. There cannot be double standards, say, between big and small countries or between those with wellknown [sic] and lesser-known languages. (*Many Languages, One Family* booklet)[1]

Linguistic and cultural diversity is a dominant feature of all EU institutions. The impact of the coexistence of several languages and the potential conflicts caused by the different administrative cultures and national loyalties are regularly brought to the fore in studies of EU administration. Multilingual practices and informal code-switching, however, only apply in the internal everyday workings of the institutions.[2] In official meetings, and especially in outside communication, it is the task of translating and interpreting, the two corollaries of multilingualism, to safeguard the ideals of democracy, transparency and linguistic equality. Building a multilingual institution where no one language is allowed to dominate necessitates that the staff numbers will be "overburdened" with translators and interpreters (Jean Monnet, cited in Stevens 2001: 126). Translating and interpreting are thus among the core functions in the EU institutions. Their relative absence in research reports and text books on EU institutions is therefore striking. For example, an internal anthropological

---

[1] Critical voices have pointed out that this proviso only applies to *national* languages, and that 'the right to know' is not extended to regional languages and linguistic minorities. The choice of official languages is, however, up to the Member States themselves (see article 8 of the regulation No 1).

[2] It is nevertheless necessary to stress that language use in multilingual communities often tends towards pragmatic choices of a few lingua francas. In the various EU contexts, the official policy of linguistic equality gives way to the use of French and English in everyday contacts (O'Driscoll 2001).

survey of the European Commission (Abélès et al. 1993) ignores translators and interpreters; an anthropology of the European Union (Bellier and Wilson 2000) only mentions them in passing, and a recent text book on the administration of the European Union devotes one page to "linguistic duties", listed just before a slightly longer section on housekeeping, repairs and cleaning (Stevens 2001: 161-162; see, however, also 125-128 on the historical background and organization of the translating and interpreting services).

Building Europe

There are a number of competing interpretations of the role and status of the EU institutions, epitomized in the role of the European Commission: some see it as a technocratic secretariat of intergovernmental cooperation, others as a bureaucratic executive force, and yet others as the political engine of a supranational entity. The more weight one puts on its independent room for manoeuvring, the more significance one has to attach to the practical realization of multilingualism. The building of the EU is not only a technical process of harmonization and integration, but also one of legitimization, and the structures and aims of the EU must find approval and meaning among its people (Bellier and Wilson 2000: 15). In her study of the EU administration, Anne Stevens (2001: 248) emphasizes the impact of the EU administration upon its legitimacy. Since that administration is multilingual, and mainly communicates via translated (or interpreted) messages, the role of translation in gaining, maintaining and supporting legitimacy is significant. Values such as transparency or democracy have little meaning unless the administration is accessible and understandable in those languages spoken by the people of Europe.

From the very beginning in the 1950s, there has been an idealist driving force behind the European institutions. When the European Coal and Steel Community was first established, its explicit aim was to guarantee that the atrocities of the Second World War would never be repeated in Europe. In contemporary discussions, the most prominent idealist component and the carrier of the peace project tradition is to be found in the idea of European citizenship. For this reason, the officials are not only serving Europe, they are *building* Europe, and to accomplish that, they need to 'introduce the citizen of Europe' (Hooghe 1997).

Introducing the citizen of Europe has not been an easy task. European citizenship is not a natural identity but an ideal the institutional discourses and practices are attempting to build. The symbols of European unity (such as the anthem, flag, public holiday and common currency), except for the Euro, are not widely recognized, and few people are emotionally attached to these symbols. Moreover, the EU institutions do not enjoy wide public popularity, and there is a growing perception of a democratic deficit. As the poor fate of the proposed European constitution in the referendums conducted in France and Netherlands in June 2005 clearly indicated, the lack of public support poses a serious threat to the EU institutions.

It has been generally agreed that a major obstacle in the building of Europe is the institutions' inability to communicate their aims to the people in different Member States. This shortcoming has not escaped official attention, and a number of (e-)initiatives have been launched to improve dialogue. The *Citizens First* programme of the 1990s aimed at informing people about their rights and opportunities in the European Union. The *Your Europe* web page now continues the same task. The need for increased transparency has resulted in a more open communication policy. The Europa portal (http://europa.eu.int) contains a massive amount of information and documents available in various languages, and includes systematic structures for direct dialogue. For example, 'Europe Direct' provides a direct link for queries about the European Union. The idea is to establish rapport, and the style is designed accordingly: when I tried the system in Finnish, the prompt response opened with an informal greeting "Hei Kaisa!". To attract the attention of the younger audience, and to tell them that 'Europe is fun!', a separate page 'EuropaGO' with games has been designed (in 11 languages). More adult citizens are invited to engage in dialogue with Commissioner Wallström who maintains her own weblog (in English).

All these new forms of interaction are related to an extensive reform of the EU governance. This change of policy line has been labelled a 'participatory turn', manifested in the increased usage of participatory speech in policy papers (Abels 2002; Bora and Hausendorf 2006). In the *White Paper on European Governance* (2001: 3), for example, it was recognized that to resolve the increasing distrust and apathy towards EU institutions and policies, the EU institutions need to "try to connect Europe with its citizens". The aims of this reform have been to involve more people and organizations in the processes, to increase openness and dialogue, to simplify and clarify EU law, to improve the Union's international representation and clarify as well as refocus the roles of institutions. Governance, in other words, is defined in terms of relationships and procedures (see also Bora and Hausendorf 2006: 29).

The participatory turn also implies new, more dialogic forms of communication. The role of communication is crucial in narrowing "the gulf between the European Union and the people it serves", in improving the consultation processes and in clarifying EU law. This issue is largely about how understandable and accessible the messages are, and how and whether they are listened to. In addition, this issue is about how and who is allowed and able to talk to the institutions, and how and whether they listen. Governance, it is explained in the White Paper, means the "rules, processes and behaviour that affect the way in which powers are exercised at European level" (2001: 8). As to how the rules and guidelines are to be defined and implemented in the multilingual communication processes, the White Paper is of little practical use. It discusses (ibid.: 4, 8) the need for "up-to-date, on-line information", "stronger interaction with regional and local governments" and "more systematic dialogue", "more clarity and effectiveness in policy execution", with scarcely a reference to the linguistic aspects of these goals.

The White Paper contains only two statements that can be considered as guidelines for translation work, although translation is not explicitly mentioned – it is not mentioned anywhere in the entire document nor is it reflected in the follow-up report on European governance (2004), except for a lament that the need to accommodate the new languages has stalled the simplification of EU legislation. Implying the need for translation, the White Paper first stresses the need to communicate more actively with the general public, and to deliver information at the national and local level (2001: 11). This information "should be presented in a way *adapted to local needs and concerns,* and be available in *all official languages*" (ibid., emphasis added). Second, it states that achieving the goal of openness requires paying attention to the ways language is used in communication. The significance of the latter statement is further enforced by its position as the very first of the five principles (openness, participation, accountability, effectiveness and coherence) of good governance proposed in the White Paper:

> The Institutions should work in a more open manner. Together with the Member States, they should actively communicate about what the EU does and the decisions it takes. *They should use language that is accessible and understandable for the general public.* This is of particular importance in order to improve the confidence in complex institutions (2001: 10; emphasis added).

The Commission's translation service does not have a stated policy line regarding translation strategies (cf. its mission statement below).[3] But if one were to infer a translation policy from the White Paper, it would be a reader-oriented one, empowering the translators to adapt the texts to local needs. This policy would also encompass all kinds of texts, not only the glossy brochures traditionally labelled for the 'general public'. The new policy of extensive on-line information is in fact rapidly erasing the distinctions: for example, since

---

[3] In 2007, at the time of finishing this manuscript, the profile of the language services was boosted by the nomination of a distinct multilingualism portfolio and Commissioner in the Barroso Cabinet. Several new documents were then issued. It was not possible to include an analysis of them here. However, regarding translation policies, the link on the web pages of the Europa postal (Europa – languages – translation – policies) as yet only contains the very first Council Regulation of 1958 (accessed 12 June 2007).

July 2004, all EU legislation has been available on-line, as are many internal staff documents. If anything, the White Paper puts forward a proactive role for the translators. At the same time, however, the implicitness and invisibility of translation in the document sends another kind of message: that of translation as a mechanical process unnecessary to dwell on when pondering the best ways to reach the people of a multilingual Europe.

The invisibility of translation and translators was further reinforced in an action plan to improve 'communicating Europe' (SEC (2005) 985) published in July 2005. The aim of the plan was to ensure "more effective communication about Europe" by introducing "a modern and more professional approach" within the Commission (2005: 2). This plan proposes a number of efforts ranging from adding competent staff in local representations to coordinating all Commission communication into a coherent action. Although the action plan stresses the need to address local audiences in their own language, it fails to make reference to the Directorate General of Translation. The plan laments the fact that "the Commission lacks communication specialists" (2005: 7), yet the approximately 1,750 professionals (the number of translators is steadily on the rise) of multilingual communication working in-house are entirely overlooked.

The overall impression one gets from these communication and language policy documents is that even though translation is a core activity, and multilingualism is praised as a core element of EU policy, the potential provided by the large in-house translator crew has not been realized, and translation remains an invisible activity perceived as a form of mechanical code-switching. The expertise of trained translators in issues such as readability, cultural adaptation and audience design remains untapped in high-level policy papers.

Legal selves in a law-based administration: Staff Regulations

Policy papers provide a high-level framework for translators' work, but they function on a very abstract level and offer limited practical guidelines. The Staff Regulations, then, provide detailed provisions for various practical aspects of both the public and private lives of all EU servants, translators included.

To accomplish the tasks they are designed to perform, all institutional settings need to construct and regulate particular 'selves' for both insiders and outsiders. Being a patient, a client, a receptionist, a police officer or a teacher requires adopting a particular behaviour and attitude. Since EU administration is largely law-based (Stevens 2001), these 'selves' are managed by legislative means. The "legal self" is "an abstract person, subject to general rules laid down by a legislature" (Hopper 2001: 130). The most significant legal document shaping the selves of the Commission translators is the Staff Regulations to which all civil servants working for the European Union institutions are subject. The Staff Regulations provide a legal basis for "all the formal events of an official career, from appointment to resignation or retirement, and for the relationship between the EU institutions and their employees both individually and collectively" (Stevens 2001: 46).

The Staff Regulations stipulate that officials are bound by a loyalty to the European Communities:

> An official shall carry out his duties and conduct himself solely with the interests of the Communities in mind; he shall neither seek nor take instructions from any government, authority, organisation or person outside his institution. He shall carry out the duties assigned to him objectively, impartially and in keeping with his duty of loyalty to the Communities. (Article 11)

What precisely the interest of the Communities is, however, remains rather vague, as does how the officials should respond to the changing political tides and geographic contours. This lack of firm grounding, it has been suggested, prevents the general internalization of moral attitudes or a specific ethos of accountability (Stevens 2001: 69). The civil servants are therefore bound by an abstract service ethos, but left to figure out for themselves what this ethos entails and how it affects their relationship to the outside world. For the translators, who often see their task as serving their readers, the European citizens,[4] the contrast between the Staff Regulations and their professional duties introduces a potential conflict of loyalties.

The Staff Regulations also provide for ample financial benefits, such as an expatriation allowance, remunerations for resettling expenses and travel costs for visiting their former home country. EU officials do not pay national tax; the institutions have their own taxation system. The benefits and support systems also include family allowances; all family members can be covered by the social security system, and practically all children of officials go to the European school founded specifically for them. Another service is a grocery shop exclusively for employees (although not nearly as luxurious as is sometimes assumed), a post office and two banks in the Commission auspices in Luxembourg. As a result, the entire family can largely isolate themselves from the surrounding society, especially (as is often the case) if both parents work for the institutions or if one stays at home. It has often been noted that EU officials inhabit a parallel universe, with few contact points with the host country (Abélès et al. 1993; Stevens 2001; Zabusky 2000). The structures, both legislative and practical, support this parallelism.

---

[4] Seven of my eleven focus group participants responded in the questionnaire that it is the primary task of the DGT to serve the European citizens; only two of them answered that it serves the Commission or the Commission officials.

4.3 Translating in the European Commission

DGT

Taken together, the European Union institutions are by far the biggest player in today's field of institutional translation, employing some 4000 translators as well as a large number of freelancers. But this is not a uniform field. The general usage of the term "EU translation" can easily make us forget the differences, and lay people may sometimes even assume that there is a single 'EU translation service', while there are in fact nine separate translation departments attached to the various EU institutions, each customized to serve the needs of that particular body. While the departments are similar in some ways, they are also significantly different. Moving between them is, as one participant in my focus group discussions described the experience, "like changing for a similar post in a different firm ... in principle you do the same work, but the environment differs, a lot". The EU institutions are different not only in location (not all of them are situated in Brussels!) and size (both generally and with respect to their translation departments), but also in their source and target language distribution and in the political and ideological rationale behind their translation policies (See Wagner et al. 2002: 14-23).

For an ethnographic study, the entire field of EU translation is far too wide and varied to be covered by one researcher. An obvious choice for me then was to narrow the focus further to the institution I know best: the European Commission. With its nearly 2000 in-house staff and its institutional role that includes both legislative activities and ample dialogue with the Member States and the general public, it is in many ways the most prominent actor in the field of EU translation. Arguably the largest translation agency in the world, the Directorate-General for Translation (DGT) serves the translation needs of the European Commission and is still an enormous entity. The yearly output of the DGT is one and a half million pages (in 2003; the figure for 2004 is slightly smaller due to a policy of demand management); prior to the latest enlargement of Bulgaria and Romania, the 25 Member States were served in 20 different languages; there were 77 translation units located in Luxembourg (Directorate A with 41 units) and Brussels (Directorate B with 36 units). Additionally, some of the staff translators were posted in the 18 field offices around the European Union (see http://europa.eu.int/comm/dgs/translation/index_en.htm).

The units and offices, while structured and constrained by the same institutional framework, are largely independent. The division is based on language: the organization chart has a separate line for each official language. These are only then further divided thematically (six units for French, English and German; four thematic units for the other 'old' languages; three for the new languages as of 2004). With little official guidance of translation policy, and with each unit comprised of just one nationality (or, in the case of languages spoken in more than one member state, a few nationalities), the structure supports the development of separate translation cultures within each unit. It is my gut feeling that this has indeed happened, but it will remain the task of further research to establish whether the attitudes and practices in other units are different from the Finnish unit under study here.

If the DGT is large, so is the Commission in general. For an individual employee, the sheer size of he Commission can be inhibiting. When I asked the translators to describe the Commission in a questionnaire that I used to gather explicit information on some practical aspects of their life and work (see Appendix 2), the one word used most frequently was "big", accompanied by "impersonal", "slow", "a bureaucratic machinery", "a bureaucratic administrative organ". These descriptions do not reflect great emotional attachment, but they are not entirely negative either: 'bigness' also implies an "international", "multicultural", "interesting" and "productive" place to work. It is also "safe", and "takes the right kinds of initiatives" (there is only this one reference to EU policy); in other words, is it a big friendly giant?

Mission

The institutional structure of the Commission translation services has undergone some major changes during the past few years. What used to be a *Service de Traduction* (known as the SdT) has now been upgraded to a full "DG" status. It is now the Directorate-General for Translation, "DGT". At the same time, the previous, separate LA-category of posts, reserved for translators and interpreters, has been discontinued, and translators are now regular A-level officials who are in no way separated from other officials in other DGs (the rights and obligations used to be the same for A and LA officials at any rate, and the change of status did not result in new remunerations for translators).

The new DGT has extensive web pages. On these pages, the mission of the DGT for 2004 (viewed 22 June 2005) is expressed as follows:

> The mission of the Directorate-General for Translation (DGT) is to meet the Commission's needs for translation and linguistic advice with respect to all types of **written communication**, to support and strengthen multilingualism in the European Union and to help to bring the Union's policies closer to its citizens, thereby promoting its legitimacy, transparency and efficiency.
>
> In 2004, the DGT strives specifically to
> make **EU enlargement** a success by incorporating the 20 official

languages into the Union's daily work and by improving multilingual communication in the enlarged Union;

pursue the Commission's strategy designed to **match the supply of and demand for translation** in a cost-effective way;

promote interinstitutional cooperation in the translation field by optimising the use of resources for internal and external translation, recruitment of staff, compilation of terminology and the development of multilingual IT tools;

strengthen cooperation with the other Directorates-General and Services of the Commission in the area of **prioritisation of documents**;

further **improve the quality** of both internally and externally translated documents and raise productivity;

develop its **role as the language service** *par excellence* in Europe. (http://europa.eu.int/comm/dgs/translation/about_us/mission/mission_en.htm; all emphasis in original)

The opening chapter of the mission statement links translation to the core values of legitimacy, transparency and efficiency. In other words, the DGT posits itself as central to the policy-making process. In what follows, however, efficiency seems to dominate: the DGT sets itself the tasks of integrating the new languages into the work flow, matching the supply and demand of translation cost-effectively, optimizing the use of resources by intra- and inter-institutional cooperation and raising productivity. All these are worthy causes, but they are rather one-sidedly devoted to the organizational and procedural aspects of *managing* the massive amount of translations as efficiently as possible. Were a translator to search for advice on how to promote the other two values (transparency and legitimacy), this statement would be less useful. The only comment related to the actual products and the individual translators' work processes and strategies concerns the aim to "improve the quality" of the translated documents. Without specifications, these are empty words, especially when they are immediately followed by the aim to raise productivity. A number of questions remain. For example, what kinds of qualities will be preferred? Are resources planned for the translators to meet the aim of raised quality? What is the quality now and how has it been evaluated? How will the aim of increased quality be met simultaneously with increased productivity? And most importantly: where is the DGT aiming at, and with what kinds of strategies? If we want to assess the quality of the end product, we need to know the yardstick. Is it a priority that the end product be linguistically correct, an accurate rendering of the original, that it be optimally readable or functionally adequate or adapted to a particular sub-audience?

In spring 2006, the DGT mission statement was revised. This revision meant that transparency and legitimacy were now elaborated at more length (viewed

12 June 2006), positing the DGT in a more central role in the communication processes of the Commission. This was a promising sign of the DGT taking a more proactive role. The aim of improving the quality of the translated documents was deleted, and the new mission statement contains no reference to the products themselves. In his plenary speech at the FIT World Congress in Tampere in 2005, Director-General Karl-Johan Lönnroth elaborated more extensively on the DGT quality assurance systems (Lönnroth 2005). The Total Quality Approach extends from the recruitment process[5] and in-house training to the workflow management systems, revision processes and translation tools. In many of these, the DGT is indeed a language service *par excellance*. But all these are instrumental factors. What was missing from Lönnroth's presentation and what is missing from the mission statements is a truly proactive approach to what translation can offer to the entire communication process and a vision of what the sought-for qualities are. The present approach to quality issues seems to be "no news is good news" (Lönnroth 2005: 33). That is, if there are no complaints from the clients, product quality is assumed to be sufficient. Instead of just relying on this reactive approach, the DGT might, for example, benefit from employing methods developed for testing the usability of techni-cal communication (for an overview, see de Jong and Schellens 2000). It is not enough to get the workflow proceeding smoothly and to meet deadlines. The entire DGT is there to communicate with the readers. If the DGT fails in this respect, advanced translation tools and swift document flows can only have limited value.

Material environment: JMO

Perhaps the most novel aspect of ethnography for translation studies is its contextualizing power. The context as such is not an innovation. It has rather become a truism to say that translations do not take place in a vacuum, that they need to be interpreted and evaluated in their relevant context. Context has been taken to include the genres and intertextual networks as well as the ideological and cultural factors affecting the production and reproduction of cultural goods. In short, ethnography takes a more material approach to the notion of context. In addition to the textual and ideational contexts, it focuses on the mundane physical settings. In order to understand the translations produced by the Commission translators, it can be useful to look at issues such as where they are physically located, and with whom, how their offices are designed

---

[5] The Commission even exerts influence on the stages prior to recruitment: it wishes to guide and inform translator training – in particular, in those Member States where univer-sity training has not been available. To that end, the Commission has drafted a model for a "European Masters of Translation" which it is now promoting (see Chapter 2).

and decorated, whether there are indications of eurospirit or mementos of their home country on the walls, and so on. Minute details such as flag stickers or table cloths, and practicalities such as the flight schedules or the location of lifts can help in creating an overall picture of the production[6] context of EU translations. The material organization of organizations can be revealing of their ideals and ideologies:

> Organizations are filled with things that cut, puncture, print, mold, ride, and drill at the same time that they denote, describe, represent, and signify. Our ambition should therefore be to grasp both aspects of their simultaneity: the materialization of ideas and the symbolic and practical aspects of things. (Czarniawska-Joerges 1992: 53)

Following the latest enlargements, all translators working for the new member states are now located in Luxembourg. The Commission translators in Luxembourg are all situated in the *Jean Monnet building* (JMO). This has made the JMO a veritable House of Translators, and other DGs have for the most part moved away. It is somehow fitting that translators are housed in the building bearing Jean Monnet's name. When the Coal and Steel Community was first established in Luxembourg, it was Monnet who did not want any one language to dominate, and he employed the first translators, interpreters and legal translators for the Coal and Steel Community (Stevens 2001: 126).

The JMO is a monolithic and quadrangular office block in the middle of the European institutions' district of Kirschberg, where, for example, the European Parliament offices, the Court of Justice, the Court of Auditors, the European Investment Bank and the European School are located. The JMO is a curious mixture of solemnity and worn-out 1970s style. Outside, its brown glass walls are impressive but also hermetic: the windows are indistinguishable from the wall, and the main entrance is hidden from view. The row of flags outside the building serves as a global symbol of international organizations; the parking lot with its rows of non-luxury family cars indicates that this is the normal workplace for hundreds of people. Beyond the revolving doors, the entrance hall is rather small and low, the low ceiling being further lowered by a decoration constructed of plastic pieces. The yellow no-nonsense information desk and the security officers block unwelcome visitors while workers hurry inside after showing their IDs.

The miniflags and displays of multilingual brochures, together with a tobacco shop selling international newspapers from all over Europe, mark the entrance hall as an international space. In contrast, when one enters further

---

[6] A similar endeavour focusing on the *reception* of, say, EU forms to be filled in by farmers would undoubtedly yield equally interesting results.

inside, the different translation units mark their territories with the help of posters depicting touristic sights of their home country, and many translators indicate their national identity by a small national flag sticker beside the name tag on their office doors. The language units exist side-by-side like neighbouring countries. Walking around the building one can make a "grand tour of Europe", as one of the translators was advised to do in a welcoming speech for new officials. However, since the corridors are typically not crowded, and translators are typing away in their rooms, in practice the tour would be more like visiting a poster exhibition.

The 1970s decorations and colours, plus the wall-to-wall carpets (actually ceiling-to-ceiling since the corridor walls are also carpet-covered) create a close to psychedelic atmosphere, especially in the conference area, where the carpet is green. Further inside the building, the corridors are more forlorn than psychedelic: the carpets are torn and dirty, the yellow file cabinets are dented. The JMO has a definitive aura of past grandeur; what was once a monument of a new spirit is now an old building in need of extensive revamping. It may still be "the heart of the Commission in Luxembourg" (Hansen 2003), but the heart is not healthy. During my stay, the translators jokingly told me how it was advisable to avoid unsettling the flimsy walls between the offices because of asbestos; a year later it was broadcasted that the trade union[7] had ordered investigations and that the employees may refuse to enter the building unless something is done to remove the carcinogenic materials found in the ceilings (*La Voix du Luxembourg* 15 June 2005). In June 2004, the feeling of a lost era was further strengthened by the number of derelict EU buildings around the JMO: the Court of Justice building had been demolished, stripped to its bare iron skeleton, and the neighbouring "Cube", which used to house Euratom, had been closed. A symbolic reading is easy: after the "messianic" work of men like Jean Monnet and Robert Schuman, and the "heroic period" of the 1960s (Abélès et al. 1993: 30), work at the Commission has turned into one of business as usual if not disillusionment, and the old generation feels that the newcomers lack enthusiasm and idealism (ibid.: 19).

The Finnish Unit

Were there any characteristic traits special to the area hosting the twenty-eight employees of the Finnish[8] translation unit? Whereas there were large photos of Finland (by Per Wolthers) on the walls, the photos were artistic rather than

---

[7] For more on staff representation and trade unions in the EU institutions, see Stevens (2001: 56-62).
[8] Since Finland has two official languages, Swedish-speaking Finns are also employed in the Swedish unit.

promotional, and Finnish flag stickers were rare. So Finnishness was not advertised, and decoration was minimal. Instead, there was another remarkable feature that immediately caught my attention: linoleum floors in offices. When the unit moved to its present location in 1997, we were all complaining about the old wall-to-wall carpets, but only those who had a diagnosed allergy or asthma were allowed to have it removed from their office room. This right had later been extended to others as well; a change of practice remarkable enough to be labelled as the "Finnish linoleum revolution". This will to actively improve the material working conditions is in stark opposition to the relaxed attitude towards the asbestos problem. Perhaps the magnitude of the problem prohibited active resistance. A wall-to wall carpet is easy to remove; getting rid of the carcinogenic materials requires rebuilding the entire complex and relocating all the employees.

The Finnish Unit is located in a far corner of the fourth floor of the JMO. It is as quiet as the other translation units, but owing to its location, this is further strengthened by the lack of commuters passing by on their way to other parts of the building. This lack of commotion was a distinguishing feature of the unit during my stay. In my field notes I described it with the help of a Finnish saying that depicts a felt boot factory as an epitome of silence:

> The Finnish unit is as quiet as a felt boot factory: everyone is toiling in their own rooms. Although the pace of work is exceptionally slow, people do not gather in the hallways or in the library room to chat. Everyone pops in [the library] to read the newspaper and tiptoes back to their room.

Translation is a largely solitary activity, and this offers a partial explanation of the subdued atmosphere. However, as I noted, the pace of work was "exceptionally slow" and the translators were not terribly busy working with their computers. The strict priority measures introduced in order to accommodate the new languages in May 2004 also affected the incoming work for the old non-procedural languages. In addition, the parliamentary elections in June 2004 and anticipation of the new Commission halted policy work to the extent that there were entire days without any new requests during my stay (see also Lönnroth 2005).

One feature that added to the perceived dullness was the amount of individual work arrangements. When I first started organizing the focus groups and offered a number of alternative schedules for the participants to choose from, I found it peculiar that very few people were willing to participate in any afternoon groups. After a while I understood that it was because they simply were not there in the afternoon: some took part in language courses, others had negotiated a part-time contract or telework arrangements for the afternoons.

These arrangements are provided for in the Staff Regulations. The employer supports and also sponsors further education (Article 24a), and translators are expected to keep adding new languages to their repertoire. Part-time work is also granted to parents of children under 12 years of age, for those who need to take care of their seriously ill or disabled family members, for further training and for the final years of service before retirement (Article 55a). Another option – telework – is fairly new and controversial. As stated in the Staff Regulations (Article 20), officials have to reside near the place where they are employed. The possibility ofr teleworking has not changed this situation. The translator working at home must be prepared to return to the office at short notice if summoned. The Finnish translators use telework for dodging the rush hour traffic and in order to be at home when their kids return from school, but even those who have made arrangements for telework mainly work at the office. Teleworking is a sensitive issue for the translation service, because it undermines the status of in-house translators: what is the point of granting translators the A-level official status (and paying for it) if they could just as well be self-employed freelancers working from home? This is why the issue is treated with some caution, as in Wagner et al. (2002: 13): "[O]ne hopes that home working will always be on a purely voluntary and limited basis".

Among the Finnish translators, there is a strong feminine bias in part-time work and teleworking. I did not hear of any men using these options, but several women did. There are family reasons behind this: the Finnish translators who were recruited *en masse* in and after 1995 were in their early thirties then and are now in their forties, and many have school-aged children. Part-time and telework help them combine family and work. Many of the men, by contrast, have housewives taking care of the home and children. Translating is often considered a feminine profession. Against this background, the gender distribution of the unit was fairly even: of the 23 translators, 16 (plus the head of unit, and all the assistant staff) were women, 7 were men. This probably reflects less the relative equality of the unit than the lucrative material benefits associated with A-level salaries and the long tradition of masculine bias in the European Commission. The old LA posts were the only A-level posts with a tradition of more or less 50/50 representation of men and women, but even in this case there has been inequality in terms of access to promotion (Stevens 2001: 111; see also Abélès et al. 1993: 21-25.)

4.4 Living in Luxembourg

Since the Staff Regulations stipulate that all officials are to reside within easy reach of the place where they are employed, living arrangements are not a free choice but an integral part of the package. Table 4.1 shows how the focus group participants responded to the question regarding which country they felt their actual (true or principal) home is located in, and whether they lived in rented houses/ apartments or had bought property in Luxembourg. The majority had settled in Luxembourg with their families, and considered it to be their home (there was no bias according to the amount of time they had spent in Luxembourg). Everyone at least had a rented apartment in Luxembourg (in other words, no one was commuting daily from neighboruing countries), but the number of staff who had bought or built a house there was slightly lower than I had anticipated, perhaps indicating some hesitation in settling down.

	Home	Renting Property in Luxembourg	Owning Property in Luxembourg
Luxembourg	8	4	4
Finland	1	1	
Lux AND Finland	1	1	
France	1	1	

Table 4.1: Where the Finnish translators feel their home is and their living arrangements in Luxembourg

The Grand-Duchy of Luxembourg is geographically, demographically and linguistically specific. Located in a small patch of land between France, Germany and Belgium, it is, as one of the respondents described it in the questionnaire, "a small picturesque spot on the map of Europe". Two-fifths of the Luxembourg population of 500,000 inhabitants are of foreign origin, representing 150 different nationalities; in the capital city of Luxembourg, their number exceeds 50 per cent. It follows that there are numerous minority languages spoken by different immigrant groups. The Portuguese are the largest community (60,000), and the Portuguese language (together with Italian) has been accorded some presence in the local schools. Other than that, the official language policy reflects geography more than demography. The complex system of trilingualism integrates German, French and the local Lëtzebuergesch language, shifting their representative status in administration, the legislative system, education and the mass media (Christophory 1998).

The unique features of Luxembourg were not decisive factors when the Finnish translators were making their career choices. As they pointed out in the discussions, they did not originally move there because they found Luxembourg such an attractive place to live in; it just happened to be the place where the translation post was located: as one translator put it, "I came here because I was offered a job here, so I live here, I have nothing against it, I like it all right, but, well, I have not even tried in any way to became local."

The "bubble" created both by the parallel universe of the EU institutions and the extensive international community in Luxembourg functions as a further insulation layer. It is thus not surprising that there have been some tensions and hiccups in the expatriates' path to becoming established residents of the Grand-Duchy. For example, during my stay, the expatriate translators closely followed the development of on-going European Parliament elections in Finland but did not vote in the Luxembourg elections that were on at the same time, nor did they seem to have much interest in finding out the latter results. They were avid readers of Finnish newspapers and magazines (both via the Internet and other venues), and many had organized a satellite connection to view Finnish TV channels at home, but only one focus group participant was subscribing to a local newspaper. Furthermore, the expatriates' discussion of their retirement plans (admittedly in the distant future for most) indicated that they had not grown roots in the Luxembourg soil – but also indicated that many had been away from Finland for so long that they felt they no longer belonged there either. (For similar findings in the European Space Agency, see Zabusky 2000; see also Stevens 2001: 133) There was a touch of embarrassment (over not living up to the alleged expectations of internationalism?) audible in the focus group discussions, but also equally bold detachment from the homeland they had not been free to choose. In answer to my question of whether it had been easy for them to grow roots in Luxembourg and whether they felt they had become a bit Luxembourgish, the immediate response was: "*Good heavens,*[9] no way! Far from it!". This was followed by general laughter.

Although the Finnish translators did not wish to emphasize their integration in the Luxembourg way of life, they had a positive attitude towards their adopted homeland. When asked to describe it in a few words, they mainly selected positive expressions: "small and nice", "good", "child-friendly", "immigrant-friendly", "rich", "international", "cosmopolitan", "safe", "lively", "a land of many possibilities", "rewarding". Only one respondent called it "home", but many others referred to different degrees of affiliation: "a place to live", "a good place to live", "becoming more and more a home", "I would not leave". Only two statements could be classified as negative: one referred to its high cost of living; the other called it "an odd society with its miniature worlds of different nationalities", pointing to a feeling of estrangement caused by the "bubble effect".

Before visiting the unit in June 2004, I had tried to imagine how the life of my former colleagues had changed over the years. I hypothesized two possible

---

[9] English in the original. There are numerous instances of switching back and forth from one language to another in the discussions. This is a trait often identified in the discourse of EU officials: they do not respect linguistic barriers (see, for example, Abélès et al. 1993: 40; Stevens 2001: 129).

developments: that they have either established more regular interaction with other Commission officials (i.e., strengthened their contacts within the EU universe), or that they have become more integrated into the Luxembourg society (breaking the expatriate bubble). Much to my surprise, neither seemed to be the case. Instead, contacts with Finland and between the Finns seemed rather to have increased than decreased. The number of Finnish nationals living in Luxembourg has risen steadily, from a few hundred back in 1996 to one thousand in 2004. The Finnish expatriate community has become stronger and more organized: there was a Finnish-Luxembourg society organizing national festivals, sports activities, mother-child clubs, etc. There was also a web-based "bun circle", delivering Finnish bread and coffee on order. Finnish newspapers are now available on-line (the Commission employees now have Internet access at work, which we were not allowed to have back in 1997), and Finnish TV channels are accessed by satellite connection. (Virtual) Finland seems to be closer than before. So is the real Finland: it used to be quite difficult and time-consuming to travel between Luxembourg and Finland because there were no direct flights, and this made the experience of working in the EU institutions quite different for Finns compared to those who worked in Brussels and could commute much more easily (especially the French, German and Belgian nationals who do not need to cut their previous ties to a similar extent upon appointment). The recently opened flight route from Tampere to Frankfurt (Hahn) with its inexpensive fares seemed to have increased traffic in both directions: the Finnish translators can now visit Finland, and friends and relatives can visit them, more easily.

The development which is visible among the Finnish community in Luxembourg is, however, in no way unique. A similar phenomenon has been identified among other nationalities working in the EU institutions as well. According to Anne Stevens (2001: 132), social networks based on national-ity have tended to strengthen as the number of EU staff has grown, and each nationality has its own groupings that are often not confined to EU staff. This is the case with the Luxembourg Finns as well. Many of them are also mem-bers of some international groups, but they also cherish regular contact with the Finnish way of life.

4.5 Conclusions

The institutional framework provided by the Commission seems divided. On the one hand, translation has been recognized and its status strengthened (e.g., the reorganization of the translation service into the Directorate-General of Translation). The recent documents on communication strategies, with their renewed emphasis on participation, dialogue and citizenship, also provide potential avenues for increased DGT involvement in text processes. On the other hand, the fact that approximately 90 per cent of the Commission's written communication originates in translations remains completely undiscussed in the documents, and translation is curiously invisible in them. The material setting adds to this invisibility: the Luxembourg translators are physically removed from other activities and placed in a building almost exclusively devoted to them. The translators may be in-house, but they are in-their-own-house, detached from other officials.

Translators respond to this mixed institutional message by making their individual choices. The range of individual work arrangements indicates a less than total commitment to serving the institution. The active presence of (virtual) Finland in the everyday life of these expatriates can also be interpreted from this perspective: emotionally, it helps keep them at arm's length from the new country of residence forced on them by the employer.

5. Institutional Identifications

5.1 European identities

The European Union is, among or even above other things, a huge identity project aimed at producing "a new breed of people", as envisioned by Jean Monnet (cited in Bellier 2000: 60). The EU is not just a set of political and bureaucratic institutions but also "an entity creating and recreating its own culture, its own sets of representation and symbols" (Bellier and Wilson 2000: 4). Efforts aimed at constructing a new European identity have included the harmonizing of government infrastructures and legislation, the enabling of free movement, and the creation of shared European symbols such as a common currency, flag and anthem.

In spite of all these efforts, it is questionable whether many individuals throughout Europe feel themselves to be primarily "European". But it has been proposed that if European identity is being formed anywhere it is formed in the ordinary activities of the workers of the European Union institutions (Zabusky 2000: 197). Among these institutions, the European Commission occupies a unique position: it is a steering body of the world's largest supra-national regime, and its task is to identify and defend the European interest over and above the national interest of individual EU countries. One might thus expect it to be among the most effective international organizations in shaping its employees' preferences and in socializing them into adopting its ideals (Hooghe 2005).

From an anthropological perspective, the European Union institutions can be seen as "microcosms" (Bellier 2000: 60). What kind of an identity do EU civil servants, the "inhabitants" of these microcosms, develop? Are they the first "new true Europeans" (Bellier and Wilson 2000: 17), with multicultural and flexible identities? Do they feel that "they belong to Europe" (Zabusky 2000: 179)? Or do they hold on to their national identities even though they participate in a comprehensive project of Europeanization in their work? Even within one institution, such as the European Commission, simple answers are not available, and competing identities exist:

> [T]he European identity to be found in the Commission does not appear as a single coherent reference but as a complex modality of identification idealistically undertaken for professional purposes. While a corporate European identity is often demonstrated by their attitudes and patterns of communication, the various cultures and identities of the commission's officials temper and alter the strongest tenets of

Europeanism in their daily lives. European civil servants have different
ways of "thinking European". (Bellier and Wilson 2000: 7)

The specific question I wish to ask in this chapter is this: what kinds of ways
of "thinking European" do the Finnish translators working in the European
Commission employ when they talk about their professional roles? In other
words, how do they negotiate between their national and European identities,
and how does their profession affect their identities? In short: what is their
professional identity?

5.2 Provoking representations with the help of focus groups

Ethnography and focus groups

Given the complexity of affiliations and cultural relations in the EU, the usefulness of exploring identity in ethnographic studies of the European Union
institutions is obvious (Wilson 2000: 139). At the same time, such exploration
is extremely complex. First, in a complex and multicultural context identities are bound to be plural. This is where the nexus approach to identification
(see Chapter 3) is useful: it allows us to account for the various cultures and
identities and the different ways of "thinking European". Second, identity,
unlike ethnic background, is not inscribed in our outlook. What we need to
be tracing is the shifting feelings of belonging or not belonging. In addition to
observing the routines of the inhabitants, probing these feelings may require
that they are actively encouraged to talk about them. Focus groups are one
way of creating discussion fora where issues related to identifications can
be dealt with (Suter 2000). A group context is also useful for probing group
identifications and interaction. Before reporting the results of the analysis of
the focus group discussions in section 5.3, I will first give an overview of the
focus group method and describe how it was applied in this particular case.
Section 5.4 rounds off the discussion of focus groups by looking at what one
particular nonverbal feature, laughter, can add to the analysis of translators'
professional identifications.

Ethnography has a strong tradition of long-term investigation and un-
obtrusive observation of "naturally occurring data", and although some
contemporary ethnographies exclude observation altogether and work solely
or mainly on the basis of written documents or open-ended qualitative interviews (see Atkinson and Hammerley 1994: 251; Silverman, D. 2001: 45),
there often seems to be a need to justify the use of interviews as a method for
eliciting data. On the one hand, the interview is mistrusted because it creates

an artificial situation and disturbs the normal course of events: "By conducting one formal interview, we are already meddling with the social tissue of
an organization" (Czarniawska-Joerges 1992: 112). However, the same is true
of observation as well: by merely entering the field we are already meddling
with the object of study.

Interviewing is one of the most accessible techniques for undertaking research in organizations (ibid.: 199), and it also provides a forum for voicing
the inhabitants' own views: "[E]nriching as the observation might be, it will
never be comprehensive without the actors' accounts, and what are interviews
if not provoked accounts?" (ibid.: 198; see also Atkinson and Coffey 2003).
The use of informants, in one form or another, is standard practice in ethnography, and reliance on interview material, whether acknowledged and planned
or accidental, is relatively common in ethnographically oriented research.
Participant observation, the corner stone of ethnography in methodological
textbooks, may be relegated to a minor position in research reports which often seem to be based mainly on data collected by qualitative interviews (e.g.,
Feldman 1991; Barley 1991; see also Van Maanen 1988: 19).

Ethnography, a process of producing and representing knowledge of a
society or social group, is by nature geared towards understanding collective
experiences. One might thus expect group interviews, focus group research
and other means of provoking group interaction to be much more commonly
used than seems to be the case. Group contexts can seldom reach the level of
intimacy that a trusting one-to-one contact between interviewer and interviewee
can optimally offer, but if the researcher's aim is to uncover shared views or
to measure the degree of group cohesion or disintegration, group interaction
can provide richer data on the social phenomena under study.

The focus group method is based on focused group interviews used in the
social sciences (see Merton et al. 1956: 135 ff.), as refined and developed by
marketing researchers from the 1960s onwards. In short, focus groups are
semi-structured and informal sessions moderated by a group leader (Carey
1994: 226). Their purpose is to collect personal experiences and beliefs on a
designated topic. Focus groups can be used to elicit qualitative data on group
meanings, shared attitudes, beliefs and life experiences, as well as on group
dynamics and group norms. They can be productive in revealing how the participants talk about the topic (word choices, argumentation); what their shared
views, beliefs and myths are (what is taken for granted; where clarification is
asked for; what is challenged); and what kinds of emotional engagement evolve
(tone of voice, atmosphere; see, e.g., Catterall and Maclaran 1997).

It is not easy, and sometimes not even necessary, to distinguish clearly
between focus groups and group interviews. In a sense, a focus group *is* a form
of group interview. In another sense, a focus group is not an interview at all
but rather a guided discussion. Its structure and its methods of moderation aim

towards a free conversation with little facilitator input. Focus groups provide an opportunity to observe group interaction. A focus group is not an interview session but a conversation on a given topic: during a good conversation people laugh, tell stories, make funny remarks, agree and disagree, contradict themselves, and interrupt one another. All this provides ample material for analysis. Group interviews and focus groups can also be seen to differ at the analysis stage, in how the researcher approaches the gathered material and in what he or she tries to uncover. According to Michael Agar and James MacDonald, the difference between ethnographic group interviews and ethnographic focus groups is that focus group material is "not in the form of explanations but in the form of exchanges among group members" (1995: 85). In other words, focus groups are not seen as a way of gathering information that would help the ethnographer to understand the local context, but rather as an organized setting for teasing out group meanings and attitudes. Focus groups offer a tangible way of probing combined local perspectives and group interaction.

In marketing research, focus groups and ethnography are often considered to be two separate methods to choose from. Putting the two together may, however, often be the most fruitful approach. When used within a holistic ethnographic framework, focus groups can provide possibilities for richer understanding, but they also presuppose prior ethnographic work: "ethnography provides broader frames of interpretation in terms of which focus group details take on added significance" (Agar and MacDonald 1995: 78). The same is true of all kinds of interviews used within an ethnographic framework. Ethnography, whether traditional or applied, is never simply a series of interviews that are analyzed qualitatively. It always involves a contextualizing drive that leads to a direct contact with the setting, and this observational or participatory fieldwork "sets the stage" and provides "the baseline of meaning" for analyzing the interview or focus group data (Boyle 1994: 163). The interface between observations and conversations or interviews is, in fact, the central locus of ethnography.

Focus groups in the translation unit

My first article on EU translation (Koskinen 2000a) was based on my own experiences in the European Commission. When I returned to the issue from a more traditionally empirical research perspective in 2002, it was my initial plan to focus on texts only. Although I envisaged a visit to the scene in my research plan, the original design had no ethnographic orientation, and the interviews were included in the plan just to fill me in on the latest developments in the *Service de Traduction*. The further my work progressed, the more its scope expanded (the original plan only contained the perspective employed in Chapter 6). The interviews became more significant, both in the research design and for me personally. Instead of (merely) gathering information, they became a valuable source of local knowledge and opinions, and a way of analytically reflecting on my own positions. This is why focus groups seemed more suitable for my purposes than individual interviews.[1] Due to my previous insider role, there was a limited need for gathering information on how things are done. Instead, I found it essential to find a method for reaching out from my personal experiences (vulnerable to criticisms of anecdotalism) to an understanding of the professional group and its ways of interaction.

I conducted three tape-recorded sessions lasting one-and-a-half hours each: the first with the two trainees who happened to be there at the time (not included in the analysis here), the second with four participants (A–D), and the third with seven participants (E–L, minus K). The unit had 23 translators (plus the head of unit, three secretaries and a librarian, all Finns). Three of the translators were absent on sick leave or maternity leave at the time the focus groups met. Eleven of those present attended the groups: four of them were men and seven women; there were 2+2 in Group 1, 2+5 in Group 2. Nine participants refused (my research had an explicit backing of the superiors, but participation was entirely up to the individuals themselves). The focus groups thus cover half of the unit's translators. But it is important to remember that those who participated do not represent the views of those who chose to opt out in any straightforward way. It is also necessary to emphasize that the analysis is not based on the focus groups alone. But it would be equally misleading to represent the focus groups as an auxiliary method, useful for triangulation purposes only. I did not anticipate too much in advance, but it turned out that the transcriptions are a significant source of valuable data. The strength of the focus groups is that they "force" the participants to put into words issues they might otherwise seldom verbalize and to discuss the similarities and differences of their opinions and experiences (see also Suter 2000).

It is sometimes assumed that focus group participants should be recruited so that they are strangers to each other and unknown to the moderator. This rule was doubly violated in my case: not only were all the participants drawn from the same unit, most of them were also familiar with the facilitator. Whether or not this is considered problematic, however, depends on what one aims to achieve. For some purposes these affinity groups are essential. Also, as Agar and MacDonald (1995) note, in actual research, groups are often formed by networking (e.g., contacting a few people and asking them to invite their friends to join in). Agar and MacDonald do not find this problematic in ethnographic research, and I think that in my case the familiarity enhanced rather than hampered discussions.

---

[1] An added methodological benefit is that while individual interviews are relatively common in translation studies, group contexts are more seldom utilized.

Familiarity also influenced my facilitator role. In many ways, I was not a good choice: as a facilitator I was inexperienced and untrained, and I did not always manage to guide the discussions in an optimal and non-obtrusive way (on the other hand, some control is inevitable). But I think that because of my background I did quite well from the point of view of fostering good and relaxed conversation and establishing trust. Commercial applications of focus groups involve big business and trained professional moderators. However, research always involves trade-offs, and some argue for trading off some professional skills to ensure that the facilitator comes from the same population as the respondents (Fern 2001: 75). In academic projects, it has also been argued that professional moderators are "not a good idea" since they are not intimately familiar with the body of academic literature on which the project relies (Morrison 2003). Whatever the professional background of the facilitator, it is important that the group can accept and relate to him or her. A peer facilitator may find it easier to establish rapport, gain acceptability and credibility, and may also speak the same language (including the same subculture slang or professional jargon) as the participants.

Setting also plays a role in establishing a relaxed atmosphere. The choice of setting is always a judgement call; in this case it was necessary to take into account the likely increase in no-shows and opt-outs if the sessions were taken into a different locale and not conducted within easy reach of participants and during the work day. The groups thus met in the unit's library room, which is used for the weekly unit meetings but is also the only recess area within the unit. Since I was looking for occupational opinions, I did not consider the location a problem, and it did not seem to inhibit the participants either.

The general atmosphere was fairly similar in the two groups, but it needs to be kept in mind that the sessions were held on two separate occasions, and the same participants, in other combinations and contexts, might have responded differently. Personal chemistry and dynamics are not constant between groups; even though the groups follow the same route, a different mix of members provides different data. In addition, significantly, I had not met the participants of the first group before, but the second group mainly consisted of my former colleagues. On the other hand, although I had not met the participants of the first group face to face before, they probably knew *of* me, and I knew of some of them, and the shared professional ground made my researcher role fuzzy in a manner similar to the second group. For example, it is a kind of standard assumption in interview situations that the interviewer asks the questions and the interviewees answer. The interviewer is not asked questions in return. In both sessions, however, these roles were occasionally reversed, both by a participant asking *me* how things were before and by my own reminiscing contributions to the discussion.

Mind map and questionnaire

To keep the focus group focused, the ebbs and flows of discussion need to be managed and moderated. The questioning route that was used in the focus group sessions was specifically designed to provoke discussion of cultural relations and identifications. I had prepared a (deliberately handmade and not too elaborate) mind map of five foci of discussions that was distributed to all participants, together with an invitation to pick up issues and open discussion on whatever aspect they found inviting. (Not a very successful strategy: in both sessions it was the task of the facilitator to initiate the moves between different foci. When one strand of discussion dried out, the group just fell silent.) There was a box that said (in Finnish) TRANSLATORS and five circles for the different foci: COMMISSION, TEXTS, READERS, FINLAND and LUX (for Luxembourg). Lines connected all the circles to the box and some of the circles with one another, and with one-word "starters" to spark off the discussion (for a translated replica, see Appendix 1).

I was not sure what to expect from the sessions, and was in fact prepared for the possibility of not succeeding in eliciting any useful data. To ensure data collection, I also designed a short questionnaire that was filled in by all focus group members at the end of the session. In addition to the basic background questions of age, education and work experience, the questionnaire consisted of structured questions on issues such as family and living arrangements, languages and media use, contacts with other Commission employees, the amount of feedback received on translations, and so on. The questionnaire also contained some open questions on how the respondents would describe the Commission, their own work and Luxembourg (for a translated version of the questionnaire, see Appendix 2). The structured format of the questionnaire elicits detailed information on a select group of issues. This information is used to supplement focus group data.

In reading the extracts of the focus group discussions and in looking at the questionnaire form one needs to keep in mind that they were not designed to be analyzed out of context; the interpretations are woven together in an interplay of observations, discussions, reminiscences, questionnaire answers and text material. Of all these, observations have the lowest priority. To begin with, my visit in June 2004 was not very long, and it coincided with a period of low workflow (EP elections; new member states). There were thus few translators busy at work at the time, and less to observe in that sense. This unexpected turn increased the importance of the focus groups. Throughout the spring, when the unit had been extremely busy, I had been warned not to be disappointed if the translators did not have time to join the discussions. The new turn undoubtedly enhanced participation in the focus groups. It was not insignificant for the translators (especially because of the low workload) that those who participated in the sessions were allowed to mark the amount of time as time spent in "other activities" in their working-time follow-up system. The reduced workload would thus have a lesser adverse effect on their personal achievement rates. This rather recently introduced system of measuring translators' input is in line with the stated aim of efficiency in the DGT mission statement of that time. It was also a hot topic among translators – the only discussion I was not allowed to follow in the section meeting was on this system and its applications. The system also came up in the question-naires as a major de-motivating factor.

Transcription and translation

The analysis of focus group discussions is sometimes based on note-taking alone. In commercial applications, this may be warranted for financial reasons (transcribing is a slow and costly process), but it seems to me that a thorough academic analysis needs to be based on (audio or video) taped and transcribed data. In the transcription process, I tried to balance analytic needs and read-ability, keeping transcription conventions to a minimum, both to save my own time and energy and also to keep the material more readable for those not familiar with the various transcription conventions, while not cleaning up the transcriptions so much that this would unduly hamper analysis. For example, pauses and overlaps are roughly marked, but their durations are not calculated, and phonetic features such as pitch and intonation are unmarked (see Table 5.1).

It is important to emphasize that the extracts of the focus groups below do not offer the reader any direct access to the discourses of the participants. Since the discussions took place in Finnish (the mother tongue of all the participants), my analysis is based on the original Finnish transcription. My task has thus been similar to anthropologists presenting the local expressions and representations in the dominant Western language, the only difference being that I share the native language of my locals. In translating the extracts reproduced here, I have tried to respect their nature as spontaneous spoken language, retaining the hesitations and false starts, but it is important to keep in mind that these extracts and the actual discussions are three moves apart: the discussion is first tape-recorded, then transcribed and finally translated. The transcriptions are also not to be used to analyze the English usage of the participants; the English extracts are my creation, not theirs. If they appear clumsy or non-standard, it is because I have tried to follow the sentence structures and formulations as closely as possible, and Finnish is structurally rather different from English.

Transcription Symbols

Emphasis	bold
Special tone of voice	italics (added info sometimes in parenthesis)
Overlap	[
Pause within an utterance	,
Interrupted speech	–
Silence in between utterances	(silence)
Indecipherable talk	(--)
Unilateral laughter	(laughs)
Shared laughter	(laughter)[2]
Added remarks	in parenthesis
Deleted material	(. . .)
facilitator	K (for Kaisa)
participants	A–L

'Others' is a shorthand for many simultaneous responses in agreement ('yhyy', 'yyy', etc.), where individual voices cannot be recognized. It does not necessarily mean *all* others, but it does indicate an absence of any simultaneous expressions of disagreement audible on the tape.

Table 5.1: Transcription Symbols

Limits of focus groups

Each method offers a particular vista to the phenomenon under investigation. While it highlights certain aspects, it also overshadows others. Each research process thus calls for reflecting on what remains unexamined. What, then, are the limits of these focus groups? What remains beyond their reach? First of all, there is the question of those who did not take part: would their comments have been completely different? Second, to what extent did the conversations reflect the actual views of the participants (i.e., to what extent did they anticipate what I, or the other participants, wanted to hear and responded to it)? And thirdly, were there dominant views or participants overriding minority opinions? (On the effects of group dynamics, see Merton et al. 1956: 148-151)

These are speculative questions. I have no way of knowing the answers for sure. Even so, there are ways of counterbalancing the deficiencies. Situating the focus groups within an overall ethnographic approach provides contextual

---

[2] In conversation analytical studies of laughing, instances of laughter are transcribed in minute detail (see, e.g., Haakana 1999). For my purposes here, these more general symbols are adequate enough.

knowledge that can be used to assess the conversational data. An additional benefit of an ethnographic observation period is that you are physically there both before and after the group sessions. This provides opportunities for individual members to discuss and reflect on the sessions afterwards, and also to add to or explain what they said in the group situation. Even though one-to-one discussions may be too personal or confidential to be included in the report, they enhance the process by providing guidelines for interpreting the group session data and guard against pushing the interpretation too far in any one direction.

In this case, the focus group process lasted quite a lot longer than the duration of the actual sessions. To begin with, all members of the unit received a one-page introduction to my research a few weeks before I went there. Then I presented the main ideas orally during the first day of my observation period, and after that, those who agreed to join the sessions signed in. During the last day of my visit I took part in the weekly unit meeting, where I had a chance to collectively thank everyone for their cooperation both in the focus groups and in general, and also to give a more detailed presentation of my project. This prompted some new and useful comments.

In retrospect, I think that even more important than these prior contacts was the fact that I was also present after the sessions. There were a number of private discussions with some participants, reflecting on what they themselves did and did not say during the sessions ("I did not want to bring this up in the session but…") and how they felt about some comments by others ("my view was quite different from the one expressed…"). I also had an opportunity to ask for further clarification on some issues discussed during the sessions, as well as to hear the views of some of those who did not participate. For reasons of confidentiality and anonymity, most of these discussions are not explicitly included in the analysis below, but implicitly they have a bearing on my interpretations.

Although participation was entirely voluntary, and agreeing to be present in the discussions thus indicated consent, I also drafted a written agreement with each participant. In addition, I promised that the translators would have the opportunity to read my analysis before publication. The process was thus designed to include two separate steps: first the sessions and their analysis, and then the participants' comments and their analysis. The translators did not respond *en masse*. The few points that were raised (related to transcription methods, my analysis of the lunchtime arrangements and anonymization of the participants) I have tried to take into account. Member checks can be seen as one triangulation method, but I want to emphasize that relative silence is not to be interpreted as a sign of agreement: the following interpretations are mine alone, and for any potential misgivings I alone am responsible. For me personally, interpreting the focus group results was an unexpectedly intimate experience: during the analysis my own position shifted back and forth between complete outsider and total insider, between the emic and the etic perspectives. This interplay hopefully produced a "third dimension" (Boyle 1994: 166), an insight neither an insider nor an outsider alone could reach.

5.3 Translation unit as a nexus of relations

Officials and translators

In the focus group discussions, the identifications and affiliations were discussed on the basis of the mind map. The five foci around the translators – Commission, texts, readers, Finland and Luxembourg – provided a general framework for the discussion, but the conversation touched upon other issues as well, whereas some of the additional pointers (such as 'officialese' or 'bureaucracy') received little attention. In the analysis reported here I have tried to locate the main building blocks that the translators used in constructing their identities during the discussion. As was to be expected, their talk encompassed numerous elements, and their identity was not one but many. In addition to their individual personal identities which were not studied and remain within their private sphere, they collectively have at their disposal the institutional identity of EU officials, their professional identity (or identities), their national identity, and their expatriate identity, and these can be strategically put forward or withdrawn from sight.[3]

In probing the identity of one professional group of any organization, it is always illuminating to explore how they see themselves with respect to others working in the same place: to what extent they have a shared organizational identity and to what extent they assert their own special identity by contrasting it with that of others. In the case of the translators working in the European Commission, the most immediate point of reference is provided by other A-level officials, who also draft the source texts to be translated. Translators provide the service, working *for* the other officials, but they also share the same A-level status and salary levels, i.e., they work *with* the other officials. The focus group material reflects this ambivalent role. The following extract of a discussion that took place in group 2 illuminates how emphatically the translators may express their detachment from other officials, constructing for themselves a distinct professional niche. According to this discourse, translators are not in fact officials at all, or in any case not "real", "special" or "actual" officials (see extract 1). There is an in-built subservience in this discourse, both projected onto the other officials and expressed from the point of view

---

[3] Limited space allows me only to touch upon social identity theory; for a thorough introduction see Hogg and Abrams (1988).

of the translators: translators do not have "substance value", and translating as a stage is seen as separate from the actual text production process.

(1)
(in response to the question of what being a Commission "official" means to them)

E:	I don't know, I do not think of myself as an official but rather as a translator that's how, **indeed**
	(silence)
K:	Yeah, but do you feel however that you are somehow in some sort of a, centre of events or in the core [or somehow –
E:	[*it is so unbelievable, utterly amazing* (sarcastically)
	(laughter)
I:	the translator doesn't have any other business, that is, nothing to do with the production of these texts other than, than, just translating so that in that sense, we are not really, we have the status of an official but in reality we are translators just as any other translators in the world
L:	I'd say we have instrumental value [–
Others:	[yhym
L:	that we do not have any substance value unfortunately, I noticed it [last summer –
I:	[a necessary evil, to the Commission
	(laughter)
L:	well not necessarily evil but also not any such special **official** in the sense that, I noticed it last summer when I took part in one of these *stages*[4] where there were many, most of them were A-level officials there were only few translators and then some of these A-officials were like, they said that that, this is such a wonderful thing this, *I love the Commission* (dramatically), that it has so many possibilities to take initiative and make, get things done, , a translator does not have this feeling that I was sort of, it opened a new perspective but one does not get to think about it **here** –
I:	I meant a necessary evil in the sense, that, well, that well, translating, when it is translated to many languages it makes the process so much heavier according to those actual officials and the politicians who **produce** the texts that we are just a nuisance, but a necessary nuisance
Others:	Yhyy

---

[4] The French word *stage* refers to a training – and acculturation – period for A-level officials in Bruges.

There is a noticeable tendency, both in this extract and throughout the focus group material, for the participants to refer to the other Commission officials in the third person plural (they), excluding the translators (we) from the group. This way of juxtaposing A-level officials and translators is revealing: in the hierarchy of offices translators *are* A-level officials. But this discourse indicates that they may find it difficult to identify with their peers, whose professional role and level of commitment to the European ideals are perhaps different from theirs (see Bellier 2000: 56).

This differentiating discourse, however, is just one of the options available for translators. They may not wish to flaunt their love of the Commission, but they can strategically employ their role as a representative of the Commission. The two discourses, one identifying with other officials and the other disidentifying, exist side by side in the focus group discussions (cf. extracts 1 and 2).

(2)

F:	well I at least just feel that I am one employee among others
G:	for me too it is that one just works here
F:	Yes
J:	but when you for example contact experts in Finland then you feel that you are a Commission official, that that it is much easier to call and disturb another official or private worker by calling that I am so-and-so from **the European Commission** and it brings [certain status to it
K:	[yeah
K:	does it also bring that, does one like need to act like an official, that does it affect that that when one introduces oneself that one is from the Commission then does it affect that one also needs to sound convincing?
J:	it adds to the convincingness
H:	no, one needs to get it out of the way in the beginning so that one can start chatting normally
	(laughter)

It seems that the institutional identity is like a cloak you can put on when necessary, to benefit from the added support of the entire institution behind you. But it also seems that there is some variation among the translators: some feel more comfortable with the cloak than others. The strength of J's position is further enhanced in the closing remark (extract 3), expressed following the general agreement that officials see translators as a necessary nuisance (at the end of extract 1).

(3)

J:	coming back to your question of whether we feel like being separate or or one part of a greater whole, **I** at least feel, now and then that I **am** part of a greater whole if I for example in a newspaper recognize that there is talk or in the radio or in television there is talk about some text the the the drafting translating of which I have participated

The emphasis on "I" and "am" places the remark in clear opposition to the generally agreed view, expressing open disagreement. It is also a response to E's earlier sarcastic comment reflecting how the translators feel they are away from the centre of action (extract 1): J at least wants to emphasize a feeling of affinity and commitment (note also that it is J who brings up the usefulness of the institutional "cloak" in extract 2). Hesitation before choosing the verb "drafting" and then quickly abandoning it for "translating" refers back to I's previous comment (extract 1) on how translators are not involved in the actual drafting process, that they just translate (cf. Chapter 6). Interestingly, this oppositional contribution is neither contested nor confirmed by the other participants. It is left to the facilitator to continue this line of discussion by asking whether they feel their work is important. The unanimous response (J, too, joins the others here) poses serious questions related to motivation and job satisfaction (extract 4).

(4)

G:	I think it depends on what you are transla[ting –
E:	[indeed
	(laughter)
G:	sometimes one feels that there is some sense in this but well sometimes one feels that, there is not much point
F:	its like 'does someone read this?'
G:	quite, quite
J:	quite, one is always a bit surprised if sometimes, someone from the department contacts you about a translation for example if there is a mistake or something else or for some other reason then, then one gets sort of startled that yes indeed, that, that this really gets read

It is no wonder the translators sometimes feel that no-one reads their texts. They have been physically removed from other officials (most DGs are in Brussels, and even those in Luxembourg are located elsewhere in the city), and there are few opportunities to meet and discuss on-going projects with the officials who draft documents or to witness meetings that take place (let alone take part in them) before a new draft version follows. Table 5.2 shows how the respondents answered the question relating to who they come in contact with in their work.

	Daily	Weekly	Sometimes	Never
Finnish colleague translators	11	-	-	-
Other colleague translators	1	3	7	-
Requesters	-	-	11	-
Source text writers	-	-	8	3
Finnish EU officials	-	1	9	1
Other EU officials	1	1	8	1
Experts in Finland	-	1	11[5]	-
Finnish language professionals	-	-	8	3
Users of translations in Commission	-	-	7	4
Users of translations in Finland	-	-	6	5

Table 5.2: Finnish translators' work-related contacts

Since this is not a quantitative study, the sample is not representative of all EU translators, but the simple statistics show a very clear tendency at least among the focus group members: they are all in daily contact with one another, indicating that this unit is a tight and collaborative community, but they have very limited contacts with any other stakeholders; they are never or seldom in contact with the source text writers, or even with the requesters, and never or seldom with the users of their products.[6] Contact with the actual writer(s) of the document(s) is also often complicated by the lack of information on who that person is: there is always a contact person listed in the *fiche de travail*, but it is often the secretary or assistant responsible for the document, and it may well be that the contact person has in no way personally participated in the drafting process.

The same trend which is visible in work-related contacts is also easily discernible in informal contacts. The questionnaire probed this by asking respondents who they had had lunch with during the previous week. Of the 55 lunches (5 times 11), 31 were shared with the Finnish colleague translators from the same unit, and only seven with other colleagues (translators

---

[5] One respondent marked two choices ('weekly' and 'sometimes').

[6] The two reported daily contacts outside the unit, one with other translator colleagues, the other with other EU officials, may be partially explained by the fact that in addition to their regular translation tasks, the two respondents were responsible for substituting for the head of unit who was on a long leave at that time. Their responses thus perhaps reflected these duties in addition to the contacts they had in their capacity as translators.

or otherwise) (17 alone or at home with the kids, etc.). In other words, the Finnish translators work together and they have lunch together. This is quite sensible: at lunchtime you join in with others, and those you regularly work with are closest at hand for company. There is also a material explanation: in the middle of the unit there is a rattling freight lift which takes you directly to the basement cafeteria, and it is commonly used at lunchtime. There is thus little chance of accidentally meeting acquaintances from the other departments on your way down to lunch.

Focusing on lunch companions may seem trivial, but in fact lunch time provides ample opportunities for observing human interaction. It has even been argued that the shifting significations of identity are nowhere more apparent than in the cafeteria at lunch time (Zabusky 2000: 192). At *Jean Monnet*, the cafeteria functions as a meeting point for all the officials working in the building. Its meeting point – or even melting pot – function is further strengthened, for example, by occasional "nationalities" weeks when traditional food from one of the Member States is served, or by visual elements such as flags used as a reminder of the many nationalities involved. In June 2004, the Parliament and the Commission decided to welcome officials from the new Member States with a tray cloth depicting caricatures of all new nationalities (funny-looking "supermen" in national costumes).

In multinational occupational settings, the cafeteria can easily be transformed into a stage where people make appearances: it is where you can show others who you know and who know you. In these contexts, sharing the table with your own nationals only can easily be interpreted as reluctance or inability to mingle with others (Zabusky 2000: 193). In my memory, the aspect of showing off was not absent from the unit. Now I saw no traces of it. The unit had moved towards increased internal integration in that they had selected one of the long tables as "their" table so that you did not need to arrive at the same time with the other Finnish translators but could still find them and join the group. The cafeteria is the locus of potential interaction, and the absence of that interaction is also significant. My interpretation of the table arrangements is that the translators no longer care for appearances and have lunch with whoever they choose to, most often with their closest colleagues from the same unit.

Socialization to the organization

It is, obviously, in the interest of any organization to socialize its members so that the goals of the organization are internalized. It is generally assumed that the socialization process is made smoother by novelty and primacy effects. The novelty effect means that initial experiences are most influential, and newcomers are likely to be disoriented and eager to conform. The primacy effect means that age and experience have an adverse effect on socialization and that young recruits with minimal prior experience are easier to socialize (Hooghe 2005). The European Commission recruitment policy supports socialization in that recruitments are mainly targeted at the lower career levels, and translators are expected to have little or no prior experience of translation work. This policy is to some extent reflected in the focus groups, with some significant exceptions. The majority of participants had had previous work experience for 0-3.5 years, and had been recruited in their early thirties, but there are also counter-examples (10, 12 and 33 years of prior work as a translator). There were two rather recent arrivals in the groups, but the average EU translator career for the rest of the group at that point was eight years.

The uneasy and distant relation to other A-level officials already indicates that socialization to the shared goals of the institution has been less than perfect. But if one analyzes organizational socialization further, can one find support for the novelty and primacy effects? Singling out the two newcomers, with one and two years of service behind them, are they more disoriented or more eager to conform than the others? In the absence of regular formal and informal interaction outside the translation unit and participation in the relevant processes, the twists and turns of the drafting process can appear totally haphazard and meaningless, especially in the beginning (extract 5; see also extract 12). Participant C is a newcomer in the Commission, participant B an experienced translator.

(5)

C:	and I just cannot fathom why the last minute changes are allowed that, that, a few words are changed and one sees clearly that the person drafting the text has become uncertain and, changed a couple of words, , and, and, and then the, the, changes are sent and I do not know to how many, , I suppose to all [languages
B:	[yhym
(…)	
B:	there is I suppose, I have sometimes heard this explanation that the texts are circulated in those, the DGs for comments, and then a number of [officials
C:	[aha, [I see
B:	[they want to leave their signature [in the text
C:	[so it is not that the writer has been having second thoughts at night...?
K:	laughs
	(B's explanation continues...)

Eagerness to conform is tricky to measure. It seems, however, that differences in educational background might equally well explain a need to show conformity (this aspect will be discussed in more detail in the next subsection). The newcomers were not the ones most critical of the procedures, but neither were they totally uncritical in these discussions. The primacy effect is equally difficult to support: if previous experiences hinder socialization, the translators with the most prior experience should be the ones most difficult to maneuver. However, in this data, they are rather among those who are often eager to support and explain the practices even when opposed by others (see, for example, J's comments in extract 14 and I's anecdote in extract 15).

My data from the group discussions supports the findings of Abélès et al. (1993; see also Hooghe 2005), that the Commission is compartmentalized into different "Houses", and that these houses have different microcultures. Problems of information flow both in and between these "Houses" have also been identified as areas in dire need of improvement across the European Union administration (Stevens 2001: 176-181). The Finnish Unit, too, is a tight social entity, and the socialization to the overall institution appears limited.

Socialization to profession: the issue of educational background

The two groups were not identical in their responses to the issue of being a Commission official. In addition to the extracts reproduced here, there are numerous other instances of similar oppositional thinking in Group 2. By contrast, Group 1 could not be provoked into anything similar. They did use similar us/them structures, and remarked on the rare contacts outside the DGT, but the general atmosphere was not heated at all, and the question of what being an official means to them only led to a short discussion of the meaning of job security for personal and family life. Instead, B opened an interesting discussion of the problems of combining institutional constraints (the role of an official) with professional translator identity – an identity project expressed as quite unproblematic in Group 2: "we are translators just as any other translators in the world".

B had difficulty finding the right words to describe the discrepancy between the professional ideals acculturated to during translator training and the completely different reality of EU translation. This difficulty attests to the severity of the perceived gulf. Since my own background is similar to B in that I have also been socialized into the translator profession in my training, I recognized the double bind immediately from personal experience and silently sympathized with B (witness my supportive grunts in extracts 6 and 8). Rather to my surprise, the other participants did not continue this line of thought, and a silence fell over the group. Prompting made little difference (see extract 7).

(6)

B:	that is, this, this is not in accordance with the assumptions made in translation theory (laughs)
K:	yes? (laughs)
B:	in my opinion, because the starting point is the, policy that that all EU texts, certain kinds of EU texts are translated into all, languages, so that, *all citizens can have access and opportunity to familiarize themselves with EU texts* which is a totally horrifying, well, amount, that it does not sort of start with the assumption that you have a commissioner giving you, so that there would be a neat and tidy situation that there would be a commissioner who has carefully considered that now I direct this text to, that this text is directed to a particular target audience, that this sort of, how should I put it? It sort of, it is turned upside down [that
K:	[yyy
B:	whole, idea, that it is not, I do not think that it is so, how should I put it, that it would be directed towards the target [audience
K:	[yyy
B:	that it sort of rather starts from these own, own needs of the institution
K:	yeah, yeah
B:	that it is a slightly, sort of, also a difficult thing

(7)

K:	how do you others feel, feel about this?
	(silence)
K:	do you agree, or are there other perspectives to this, readers?
	(silence)
C:	hmmm
K:	text users?
A:	well perhaps, generally, speaking, well I do not really too much, often, come to think about it

Later in the discussion B returns to this issue, again supported by me. While we struggle to find the right way of expressing how we feel, C's comment singles us out as different from the rest. The impeding conflict is, however, alleviated both by shared laughter and by D's balancing response (extract 8). (The functions of laughter will be discussed in more detail in Chapter 5.4 below).

(8)

B:	in the beginning it did disturb me terribly because of my translator training, that it **is like this**, and **nothing** is specified in the request
K:	that how would one according to the skopos theory...?
B:	that this is kind of an unorthodox practice, oh well no but, somehow one begins to, not really become numb, but one kind of starts to accept [it, that, ,
K:	[yyy
B:	that it does not go as it should, or as, ,
K:	as one was taught?
B:	**yes**, sort of
K:	or as, as, yeah
B:	as in an ideal, case
C:	knowledge increases pain, , for me it has only crossed my mind that I wonder how –
	(laughter)
D:	but it is undeniably easier to translate for example a text where an internet competition is set up for school kids, you know that they are of this [or that age
B:	[**yeah, yes**
D:	this group, and of course you select the register and everything accordingly, of course it relieves the pain
	(laughter)

There is an obvious explanation for the divided attitudes: apart from B and myself, the other participants of Group 1 have a different educational background. This may explain why the issue we had found so agonizing left them nonplussed. They had perhaps never been exposed to target-oriented translation theories to begin with (see also Pym 2000: 12). Considering the fact that translator training has been well-established in Finland for decades, the number of translators with formal translator training is surprisingly low in the unit. The educational background of the focus group participants is shown in Table 5.3 (the distribution is about the same for the rest of the unit).

Within the institutional framework, translators form a distinct professional group with a clearly defined institutional task of providing multilingual documents. Behind this apparent unity there is, however, a variety of professional identities that the Commission translators had already acquired as part of their education. This variation is actively promoted in recruitment. It is a conscious policy in the EU institutions not to require formal translator training but to recruit people with expertise in a variety of areas. The only formal requirement is that the candidate must have a university degree and can demonstrate ability to translate from a number of languages in specific tests (see also Lönnroth 2005). In this unit, the policy may have resulted in trained translators being under-represented (with respect to the supply of potential candidates from translator training departments in Finnish universities) and to translator posts being occupied by linguists rather than engineers, doctors or chemists.

Linguist (foreign languages or Finnish)	5
Translator training	4
Jurist	2
Other	2

Table 5.3: Educational background [7]

The socialization of the jurists is an interesting question. Within the institutional system there is a separate professional group of "lawyer-linguists", who are hierarchically above the translators in that they have the final say in all translations of jurisdiction, and are physically separate from the translation unit (in Brussels). Jurists employed as regular translators thus face a number of challenges. First, their professional status, and salary level, is lower than that of the jurist-linguists, which may be a problem for them on a personal level. Second, they may worry about maintaining their employability as lawyers if they work as translators for too long (that is, their professional employment clashes with their professional socialization acquired during education). Third, the lawyer-linguists are often seen by translators as being too fastidious, and regular translators with legal education may need to emphasize that they themselves are not similarly fastidious. In extract 9, as a response to a question whether there are differences between the Commission translators and the jurist-translators working in the European Court of Justice, one of the jurists tells an anecdote a colleague had once told. The anecdote focuses on the thorough attitude often associated with jurist-linguists.

The recruitment policy makes sense from the point of view of the varied subject matters dealt with in the texts, but it may be less successful from the point of view of developing new practices and adapting to new demands. If there are few people familiar with translation theories in the DGT, there is perhaps also little interest in following developments in translation studies and its neighbouring disciplines. Studies of the localization processes in the

---

[7] The total is larger than the number of participants because there are two respondents with two degrees each.

IT sector, for instance, might offer new insights for readjusting and remodel-
ling the translation services (in particular since the latest developments of
introducing a separate "localization" activity in the DGT field offices in 2007)
(see, e.g., de Jong and Schellens 2000).

(9)

A:	then it is a good example that one colleague was once pondering whether 'necessary' should be translated as 'tarpeellinen' or 'vält-tämätön' and both versions could be found in translations and, after consulting the court of justice it turned out that someone there had written an entire book about this

Judging from the questionnaire answers, the Finnish unit for one is not
remarkably dynamic or driven to change. When asked to organize a number
of guiding principles of translation in order of importance, the participants
were in perfect harmony about one item: the non-importance of renewing the
textual practices used in the Commission. This was considered such a low
priority issue that three respondents did not give it any ordinal number at all,
and seven of the others put it last or second last on their lists (one placed it in
5th position). The average figures are shown in Table 5.4

1.	producing a fluent and readable text
2.	making sure that the content is equivalent to the source text
3.	keeping to the schedule
4.	adapting the text for the Finnish readers
5.	using correct language
6.	following established formulas
7.	renewing the textual practices used in the Commission

Table 5.4: Priority of factors affecting translation decisions

It may well be that the items were interpreted by the respondents differently
from the way they were originally intended, and there is no reason to draw
any dramatic conclusions based on the listing – especially since the opposite
priority of *keeping to* established practices is considered equally unimportant
and relegated to the second last position. But a certain conservativeness is
also compatible both with the subordinate discourse of translators not having
any business other than providing a translation service (extract 1) and with
the general subdued and slightly spiritless atmosphere that prevailed in the
unit during my stay (see Chapter 4). There is, however, no evidence of any
notable difference between the responses of those with translator training and

those without such training in this sample. Additionally, in a private conversation, one participant maintained that those *with* translator training are in fact more dogmatic and resistant to change than those without. It would be an interesting object of research to find out whether translators with a history of "exposure" to translation theory tend to experience a conflict between theory and practice or whether they also adopt translation strategies that are different from those of others.

Readers and readability

If there seems to be an apparent contradiction at the bottom of the priority list (Table 5.4), there is another one at the top. The first two items of the list illustrate the double bind present in all translation: there is a need to simultaneously reach towards the target text readers ("readability") and to remain faithful to the source text. Readability and fluency were given top priority, but the fact that adapting the text for Finnish readers was only placed in fourth position indicates that there are limits to the efforts taken in the name of added readability, however "unorthodox" this may be from the point of view of target-oriented translation theories. When asked whether the translators employ practical strategies to improve the texts stylistically or structurally, their responses included a lot of hedging: "I think it [rewriting] is limited to the level of two, max three, sentences", "it is different from companies where you can completely rewrite a leaflet text", "it is not really editing" (see also Chapter 6).

In the context of the European Commission, the weight of the translating institution and the relative detachment from the target audience add their particular flavour to the situation. As we saw, translators are prone to detaching themselves from the institution they work for, but the institution still imposes its own logic of communication on them. On the other hand, the translators feel they are there to serve their Finnish readers,[8] to produce readable texts for their Finnish audiences (extract 10).

(10)

G:	well yes, if it is a text that is for the Finns, sometimes they, for example I have translated texts where there were the educational systems in different countries, one could clearly see that this is not for any officials but for ordinary people, well then I do think of it from the point of view of how do I write this so that a Finn will understand and it looks nice

---

[8] The majority of focus group participants (7/11) saw it as the primary task of the Directorate-general for Translation to serve the European citizens.

K:	yeah
G:	and in that situation I feel I am, sort of, in the service of the Finns, that I try to make that, jargon, readable

This point of view is in line with translators' professional identity, with EU translators identifying with translators working in other contexts (extract 11).

(11)

I:	but isn't it so that a translator **always** thinks about the receiver, always about the reader
J:	yyy, yhym
I:	it is well, the translator's relation is precisely to the reader of the [translation
J:	[yeah, yeah
I:	so that, it is done, for the readers of a language

If the translators are willing to place such emphasis on readability and want to see themselves as serving the European citizens, why does the practice seem to be so far from the ideals of target-oriented translation theories, and why is there so much bad press on the quality of EU translations (in particular, for its incomprehensibility and poor readability)? The focus group discussions offer three explanations: first of all, translators cannot take the prospective readers into account if they do not know who their translations are directed to (see extract 12).

(12)

C:	I think that is precisely where the problem is that when you do not know who it is that in the end reads these texts, then it is, is is, difficult to ponder how –
B:	and does the writer know it any better? Probably not
C:	quite
B:	quite, that is the point
K:	yeah
D:	and does the writer remember to tell?
B:	**quite**, quite, indeed. Well that does not, it does not happen that they would tell, or it says 'general public' in the *fisu*[9]
	(laughter)
(…)	

---

[9] *Fiche de travail* is a folder accompanying the text to be translated (indicating language deadline, requester etc. – and sometimes the intended audience, as in "general public").

A:	as I said I do not, if I were to think about the target audience which I too do not often do, well, there is a big obstacle in that, that, one does not know what happens to the text after it leaves me and, how many rounds will it circle in some, procedure, before it even ends up in front of this Finnish, reader, and when it does end up in front of the Finnish reader then who that Finnish reader is, that is it some official in a government office or is it, the man in the street or who is it.

The concept of the "general public" was repeatedly referred to in both groups, and there seemed to be an agreement that texts directed at this particular audience need to be translated in a more reader-friendly manner. It is, however, not an easy task to define which documents are read by the general public and which are not. One participant raised this important issue of intended versus actual readers: "who for example has access to CELEX,[10] can the general public access it and are these directives published in the official journal?". One can discern a certain lack of information on the process in the comment (cf. extract 5), but it is also an important reminder that our information society may render many documents accessible to readers far beyond the initial or primary intended audience. This is very much the case in the EU institutions. In addition to specifically designed brochures and information leaflets (which may in fact seldom reach their intended audience), many members of the "general public" have easy Internet access to a multitude of EU documents. The EUR-LEX database (www.eu.int/eur-lex/en) contains legislation, case-law, white and green papers, reports and so on.[11] One may well want to design the translation according to the needs of a more limited intended audience, but in practice the "general public" actually has access to most of the documents (see also Tomasi 2003). For the intended transparency effect of the Internet portal to be realized, *all translations* should in fact be produced with this "general public" in mind.

---

[10] An on-line resource of legislation prior to IATE.

[11] It also contains the parliamentary questions to the Commission, and the answers provided by the members of the Commission. These answers (QEs, as they are commonly called) are translated by the in-house translators. They are an interesting genre because of their low priority in the unit. QEs are normally short, and written in simple and non-complicated language, and there are never several versions. As such they are considered fill-in jobs between larger assignments, "rehearsal material" for trainees, and also unimportant enough for the highly valued revision process to be sometimes skipped in their case, as some translators privately confessed. However, it has also been argued that the concise and deliberately allusive or elliptical nature of the answers, and the sometimes delicate nature of subject matters, makes these texts "among the most challenging of all" (Fraser B. 1997: 162).

The second explanation for the lack of reader-orientedness relates to problems of feedback. It is difficult for the translators to know how and whether they have succeeded in meeting the needs of their readers if they do not get any feedback on their work (apart from their own internal revision processes). To my question of whether feedback has increased during the years, the sarcastic reply was: "what feedback?", followed by shared laughter. (Lack of feedback and appreciation, as well as a feeling of isolation, were also regularly listed among factors affecting work motivation in the questionnaire.) What is perhaps most telling is that the translators seem to be able to identify each singular case of feedback (see, e.g., extract 13).

(13)

A:	and when I had sent it [a legal translation concerning a new Primus igniter] forward then an engineer called me from Brussels and there was a, one had to sort of invent a new name for the apparatus because no such thing had existed before and well he had been quite happy with it (laughs) I don't know who reads it in Finland but that is really for me the only concrete situation when someone has directly contacted me

The third explanation is related to the ways in which the translating institution directs the translation process. In the European Commission, institutional guidance and feedback do not support readability: the translators only get thank you notes from requesters if they manage to meet a short deadline or manage a long translation within the prescribed schedule (perhaps this is why the translators listed keeping to the schedule as their third topmost priority (Table 4.4); it is the only thing they are somewhat regularly praised for), but otherwise the rare feedback seems to focus on translating individual terms. The distant relations between translators and requesters/writers/readers may be specific to this institutional setting, rather than a feature of all institutional translation, even in the EU context. It came up in the discussions that in other institutions the relations may be different (extract 14).

Both focus groups were conducted in an amenable atmosphere where contesting views were seldom expressed and most contributions were followed by grunts of agreement or shared laughter from all or some participants. The few occasions of open disagreement are therefore particularly interesting. In extract 14, one can see speaker I getting agitated by J's way of defending the Commission practice (see also extract 3 above). But J's comment in fact confirms I's point: if there is an official – or unwritten – system of avoiding direct contact, and if you only call direct if you **have to**, the relationship is obviously more distant than when you are encouraged to call whenever you have a problem.

(14)

I:	I used to be in [another EU institution] before and we had there a much closer relationship to those, those, actual, committee members that is actual text users and producers and, and, politicians we had their e-mail addresses and telephone numbers and, and well if we had translation problems we could directly contact the commission, erh, committee members. Here it, [one cannot imagine [that –
K:	[yhyy [yhyy
J:	well one can do that [though –
K:	[do you –
I:	[(aggressively) Do you contact Prodi?
J:	well not Prodi, since I have not translated Prodi's texts but well indeed (laughs)
	(laughter)
J:	indeed I have contacted a requester [directly (--)
K:	[ycah
J:	if there was a mistake in the original or, or else, something else to ask, that we have got this official bureaucracy that you do that via file or note but that is sometimes slow and in some situations you have to call, directly, and there has been quite reasonable feedback then

On one other occasion there was open confrontation: during a discussion also related to the institutional framework and the extent to which it is allowed to dictate translation strategies. In extract 15, speaker I shares an illustrative anecdote of the true status of readers in comparison to the institutional forces in a situation where the aim of readability collides with institutional practices (cf. I's comment in extract 11). This anecdote, and the following discussion on the strange-sounding terms that just need to be used because that is how a certain concept is expressed in EU legislation, provoke H (with backup from J) to disagree openly, putting I in an underdog position by constant overlap.

(15)

I:	there was one quite interesting case, it was a pharmaceutical text, it was, well, Liikanen's[12] text in English, it was sent it was meant, Liikanen was supposed to present it, well, as a paper in some pharmaceutical conference in Finland, and well-, I trans-, I sent the draft translation to the conference organizers the experts in Finland, for them to see that, that the terms are correct and so on, and they made quite heavy-handed corrections, they put in the terms that are used in the field, field in Finland, but I could only accept part of, of, the changes because well **those** terms that are used refer to [other Commission and EU, EU documents and the terms had to be the same –
L:	[yhym
(…)	
H:	there is such a number of [genres
J:	[yes
H:	that one hardly needs in a kind of, general text that is directed to everybody then necessarily talk about 'markkinoille saattaminen' ('placing on the market') that one can quite easily talk about marketing [or selling
J:	[yhyy
I:	[yes but, hrrrm –
H:	and buying and so on but in some other places it needs to be if it has been decided upon that this is how it is expressed in legislative language [then
J:	[quite
H:	it is the way it is [there
J:	[yhym
I:	yes but it is [then in Finland
H:	[I do not think there is anymore so much of this, this anyway, the burden that, there is only one way of [expressing things
J:	[yes, yes yes
H:	that 'ainoastaan' is good and 'vain' is bad[13] and –

[12] Erkki Liikanen was the Finnish member of Romano Prodi's comission 1999-2004.

[13] These two synonyms both mean 'only', but only the first one was accepted as a correct equivalent in the Finnish EU translations ('vain' is slightly more colloquial, but the difference is not remarkable).

I:	but well here it is, in our legislation it says 'markkinoille saattamista koskeva lupa' (marketing authorization) –
H:	so it says yes, but [one does not need to
I:	[In Finland when they make [a law –
H:	[in a press release one can write, it can be 'myyntilupa' (selling permit)
I:	yes, yes, but well if one refers to, if one in Finland refers to the law that discusses these same things there it says 'myyntilupa' and not 'markkinoille saattamista koskeva lupa'

To understand the role of the translators in the European Commission, one needs to understand their ways of dealing with the question of readers. Limits to readability and target-orientedness also delineate the freedom of movement afforded to and assumed by the translators. These limits are also thus a zone of struggles of competing translation ideologies and translator identities. There is no end in sight for this competition: the fundamental contradiction between serving the two clients, those ordering and paying for the translation and those using the translated text, creates an ambiguity that goes to the heart of not only EU translation, but the entire profession of translators.

Transnational expatriates

It is a special trait of EU translation that taking up a position as an in-house translator also entails taking up residence in Brussels or, as in this case, Luxembourg. It is somewhat paradoxical that these transnational professionals, who have built a home in the multicultural and multilingual environment of Luxembourg and work in an international and multilingual institution, are actually working in a predominantly Finnish atmosphere. This is in dire contradiction with the melting pot view of the EU institutions which are often seen as a "multicultural if not Babelian world", and "a 'laboratory' where officials, recruited from all member states, commit themselves to serve 'Europe'" (Bellier and Wilson 2000: 17). While Commission officials interviewed in an anthropological study expressed feelings of "being cut off their roots" and "living in a golden cage" (Bellier 2000: 66), the Finnish translators in this study rather emphasize their continued affinities with the Finnish language and culture. Their life, according to them, is not nearly as exotic as an outsider might assume (extract 16; see also extract 18).

(16)

A:	it has not been a great leap
C:	and the fact that this, Finnish unit is so big here so that one does not and, and I at least do not actually have any contacts with the translators of other languages so in principle, and at home I have got a Finnish wife and a baby so that, at home I speak Finnish all the time and there is nothing that would betray that we are in fact abroad other than that there are no Finnish TV channels
B:	yhym, and even that is quite possible –
	(laughter)
B:	it can be organized
(…)	
C:	and then the fact that at work – oh well, at lunch you need to say a few words in French
	(laughter)

The monocultural reality of the translation unit is very different from the view many outsiders have of working in the Commission: instead of continuous contact with more than twenty different nationalities and numerous languages, the Finnish translators work with other Finnish translators and use Finnish all the time. It may, however, be that during the decade many of these translators have spent in Luxembourg they have become more acculturated than they are willing to admit – it is just not the national culture of Luxembourg but that of the international community residing there. Their neighbours represent numerous different nationalities, and so do their friends – but few of both are native Luxemburgers. At work they may have their own little Finnish corner, but outside the Commission there is no Finnish ghetto or Little Finland where they would spend their free time in an all-Finnish environment. It may well be that some of their Finnish customs have given way to a "European" code of practice (see extract 17).

(17)

G:	I have noticed then, in Finland (. . .) that I have started chatting a lot where ever I need to run an errand, it is for me at least a new characteristic (laughs)
H:	yeah
G:	I did not, before, when I lived there, do that
H:	and sometimes one can accidentally greet some unknown [passer-by
L:	[yeah
F:	(ironically) *oh no, that is a big mistake*
E:	or nod

H:	or nod at least, or even say [something
F:	[good [afternoon
H:	[and one can even slip *moien*[14]
	(laughter)

Everyday life is everyday life anywhere in the world. It is, however, obvious in the discussions that there is in the translators' discourse also a need to emphasize the monotony and lack of glamour in their life style. This defensive tendency may have its roots in previous outside comments on the affluent life of EU officials (see extract 18).

(18)

E:	sometimes my pals then in the beginning were like, *ooh, oh well,* there in *Europe,* with all the *possibilities,* (dramatically) but yeah, it is so fabulous, we go to the grocery store and, then to work and back home, that –
	(laughter)
L:	terribly fancy
H:	that it is so handy for traveling [around –
E:	[quite (laughs) indeed, it is, terribly handy, we have not [been anywhere
H:	[[(ironically) *and we have been traveling, indeed*
	(roaring laughter)
E:	I have really not been to **anywhere** in particular
	(laughter)
J:	so that we are living an everyday life

5.4 The role of laughter

As many of the extracts in the above section already indicate, there was a lot of laughter among the two groups. I did not pay too much attention to it at the time, but when I started the transcription process, the effect was overwhelming. It felt like the tapes were full of laughter. At first I mainly paid irritated attention to my own laughter, but I soon realized that I was not the only one. There are numerous instances of both shared and unilateral laughter, by myself and by the others. It is not easy to count the number of occurrences of laughter (when does one instance of laughter end and another one begin in the flow of conversation?), but an indication of its pervasiveness in the discussion is that

---

[14] 'Hello' in Luxembourgish.

extracting all segments with one or more instances of laughing into a separate file resulted in a file half the size of the entire transcription in both groups. That is, half of the time there was some amount of laughter in the air. It is such a dominant feature in the discussions that it merits closer analysis. Who is laughing, for what, with whom and why?

Laughter is a complex phenomenon, and the functions and uses of different types of laughter in particular instances would be difficult to ascertain without recourse to in-depth conversational analysis of each extract. In the following I have a more modest aim: I wish to show that laughter plays a substantial role in the discussions, and that it can be used as a tool in analyzing interaction.

A typical picture of laughter is that it is something we share with others, and that it is born out of something "humorous" (e.g., Hatch 1997). While it is no doubt the case that we often respond to joke-telling with laughter, the phenomenon is more complex, and laughter is not only a reflex response to humour. A closer look reveals a complex picture: laughter can be both shared and unilateral (i.e., one laughs but the others do not reciprocate), and shared laughter can be volunteered or invited (speakers can invite laughter by starting to laugh themselves). The functions of laughter are similarly varied. In addition to simply being a response to jokes, funny stories and witty remarks, laughter is a resource that can be strategically employed in interaction, for example to ease a delicate situation or hide embarrassment, to create a feeling of mutuality, or to single someone out (see Haakana 1999; Holmes 2000). Each type would warrant a study of its own. For our present purposes, the focus is on the interpersonal aspects of laughter, which can be a rich source of insight into group interaction:

> Through laughing, and laughing together, we contribute to the ongoing creation, maintenance, and termination of interpersonal relationships. We also display, read, and negotiate identity. (Glenn 2003: 2)

Laughing together

Instances of shared and reciprocated laughter are predominant in both sessions. Although laughter is often invited by one of the participants, typically by laughing alone within or at the end of their turn, it is almost always reciprocated by others joining in and laughing along. Sometimes communal laughter can constitute a major part of communication. In extract 19, for example, there is little new information in any of the turns following H's punch line, but each turn contributes to keeping the shared laughter alive. These jointly constructed instances, indicating a willingness to extend the humour, have been identified in other workplace settings as well (Holmes 2000).

(19)

(on the shared habit of reading the most important Finnish daily newspaper, *Helsingin Sanomat,* every day)

K:	do you feel you have to do it, that it is sort of part of this, an obligation, that comes along this work or is it more related to you own free time and also to your Finnishness?
H:	well it is luckily not an obligation, if it was one would not get it done
	(laughter)
K:	one would not do it then (laughs)
L:	one would not do (laughs)
I:	if it was an obligation one would hardly do it first thing [in the morning
H:	[yeah
	(laughter)
E:	one would postpone it (--)
	(laughter)

One basic social function of humour and laughing together is to create and maintain solidarity and contribute to social cohesion at work. Shared humour emphasizes shared norms and common ground (Holmes 2000: 167). It has thus been argued that laughing together indicates group involvement (Hatch 1997) and that affiliation is accomplished by laughing together (Haakana 1999: 109-117; Glenn 2003: 30). One could thus infer that these focus groups, with their high frequencies of shared laughter, have high involvement levels and close relations. This interpretation is further strengthened by a related recurring feature: there are numerous instances of two or more members jointly constructing an argument by taking turns in moving it forward and supporting one another's views. In extract 20, for example, D and B make a point together and in harmony, so that they take turns in giving backup to one another, and B finishes the sentence that D started.

(20)

D:	And then of course a fairly big amount of them [the texts] were [published so
B:	[quite
D:	that was also one reason why they [were then
B:	[yhym
D:	in the early years so much polished [–
B:	[indeed then in the beginning [in particular

D:	[quite
B:	so that very much attention was paid on how should I put it read-ability and, , clarity
D:	yes
B:	yhym
D:	yhym

Jointly constructed arguments and repeated occurrences of shared, some-times roaring, laughter indicate amicability. But amicable behaviour, it is necessary to keep in mind, is also a strategic choice, not just a natural state of affairs, and focus group sessions are not natural discussions but events where the participants also "pose" for the researcher. If the general tendency is towards shared views, it may encourage those with different views to laugh along, not airing their disagreements. On the other hand, laughter can also indicate potential problem areas, since it is one way of displaying that the speaker wishes to cushion a delicate issue (Haakana 1999: 220). Unilateral laughing within one's turn may be used as a cushioning device in contesting an expressed view (see, e.g., J's turn in extract 14, where J is then supported by others who reciprocate with laughter), or in expressing criticism directed either outside or inside the DGT (see extracts 21 and 22).

(21)

E:	and then sometimes the experts in Finland give us totally peculiar (laughs), well suggestions that they definitely want us to use

(criticism against the Finnish experts)

(22)

H:	some of the formulas in legislative language are still fairly stiff, they are sometimes (laughs) difficult to write down but it is going all right now

(criticism against institutional text practices; see also extract 6)

An analysis of all instances of laughter shows, however, that in both groups the vast majority of laughter is shared, and invited laughter typically reciprocated. Most occurrences of laughter which do not fall under these cat-egories in fact single out the one person who is not a member of this group and has a special role in the sessions: me. I am laughed at – gently – when I fail to produce a correct term for an institutional practice (such as "collation meetings") or misinterpret a joke; the participants use laughter as a softener when they find it difficult to respond to my badly formulated question, or they respond differently from what they expect me to wish to hear (see extract 23; cf. extract 6).

(23)

K:	how do you feel about these texts? , , are they, is it motivating and easy to translate them or are there some complicating features?
	(silence)
E:	that is a big question indeed
	(laughter)
F:	where to start?

There are few instances of unreciprocated laughter in the sessions, but even where laughter is not reciprocated, this does not necessarily imply that an opportunity for engagement is being declined (on the complexity of responses, see Haakana 1999: 57-59). In some cases the discussion just continues, but there is no indication of any opposition to the laughing person by others. There is only one case of open distancing, or even reproof, connected with laughter, and this is caused by my laughing. In group 1, I mistakenly interpreted one comment in a sarcastic frame which the speaker did not intend, and, being eager to boost a friendly atmosphere, responded with laughter. My mistake was immediately corrected (see extract 24).

(24)
(commenting on the accepted and forbidden translations for "should" in different EU institutions; cf. subchapter 6.3)

C:	and, and, well these are all of course, in my opinion these are all grammatically correct Finnish , , someone else can of course see this differently but but well it is then just that, , when you come to a new place you always need to clarify what is prohibited here and which which words are to be used
K:	Laughs
C:	which may seem a bit funny at first but one does then when one hears the reasoning then, one does understand why

In general, my own laughter is most predominant at the beginning of the first session, for two fairly obvious reasons. First, it implies nervousness and uncertainty in a situation where I felt ill at ease. Second, it aimed at promoting a relaxed atmosphere and suggesting that the discussion need not be taken terribly seriously. The supporting function continued throughout the discussions: whenever someone invited others to laugh, I was quick to reciprocate. An analysis of laughter reveals both my strategy of fostering a feeling of closeness and amicability, and also the limited success of my posture as a member of the group. Laughter delineates my researcher position in a visible, or in fact audible, way.

Laughing at ambiguities

During the sessions, all foci on the mind map were laughed at: the participants laughed at the Commission bureaucracy and its textual practices, EU officials, (the lack of) feedback, EU texts and translation strategies; they laughed at their own role within the Commission and at their (few) contacts with others; they laughed at their relations with readers, their contacts with Finland and their relations to their adopted homeland and its people and languages, and they laughed at their own ways of behaviour and at their and their family's future plans. Why did this pervasive and all-encompassing feature not draw my attention at all before the transcription process? The answer is so obvious that it is almost elusive: perhaps there was nothing exceptional in it. Laughter is a basic element of our normal everyday interaction. In his famous treatise on Rabelais and carnivalesque laughter, M.M. Bakhtin (1965/2002: 8) argues that laughter, in all its different forms, became a basic form of expressing folk cultures and world views. Analogically, laughter in focus groups can be interpreted as a way of expressing the culture and world view of EU translators.

According to Bakhtin, carnival laughter is, first, not individual but shared; second, it is universal and directed at everybody and everything, including the participants themselves; and third, it is ambivalent. It is joyous *and* ironic, it agrees *and* denies, it shows respect *and* dethrones simultaneously. This is an apt description of laughter in the focus groups as well. The most salient aspect of most instances of laughter in both groups is ambivalence. There is a theoretical link between humour and contradiction (Hatch 1997), but humour and laughter are also a way of coping with ambivalent or ambiguous situations. Individuals experience ambiguity if either the structure of their work is ambiguous or they hold multiple beliefs about a problem (Meyerson 1991: 133). Ambiguity is different from uncertainty in that whereas uncertainty can be resolved by gathering more information, ambiguity is more permanent. It occurs when a phenomenon or situation opens up two or more contesting interpretations simultaneously (Feldman 1991: 146).

Although few organizational studies have focused on laughter (Martin J. 2002: 81), an analysis of spontaneous humour and laughter has sometimes been employed precisely to identify points of ambiguity and contradiction. The results of an analysis of instances of humour in managers' meetings (Hatch and Ehrlich 1993; Hatch 1997) and of social workers' perceived ambiguity in hospital settings (Meyerson 1991) indicate that feelings of ambiguous identity or a sense of being caught in the middle can be relieved by resorting to humorous or cynical remarks. The managers are located in between their superiors and their subordinates; the social workers have to negotiate between their occupational ideology of care and the dominant ideology of medicine in health care contexts. Similar ambiguities of identity and feelings of split loyalties are discernible in the context of EU translation.

One can argue that ambiguity is a core element of translators' professional identity in the European Commission, and laughter is both an indication of these ambiguities in discussions and a coping strategy in the face of unresolvable dilemmas (see also Holmes 2000: 169). Translators' ambivalent attitude towards other A-level officials (and a tendency to exclude themselves from the group) and a feeling of being "a necessary evil" are alleviated by laughter. Laughter also cushions the discrepancy between professional ideals and institutional reality, and softens discussions of textual practices which may well seem inexplicable to outsiders. According to Meyerson (1991: 139-140), in hospital settings social workers must embrace contradictory beliefs to maintain their legitimacy, and they need to negotiate their position "on the fringe" of the institution. Similarly, there is an unresolvable contradiction between the professional ideology of translators and that of the institution for which they work. It is, as one of the social workers put it, a question of being "in the institution but not of it" (ibid.: 140).

There is ambiguity in translators' relations with the institution, but there is also ambiguity in their attitudes towards Finland and Finnishness on the one hand, and Luxembourg and their expatriate status on the other hand. Difficulties of integration in the Luxembourgish way(s) of life, the discrepancy between the alleged glamour of being a highflying EU official and the normal everyday life as well as the overwhelming Finnishness of working life within a multicultural institution are all dealt with humorously. One might assume that this kind of acknowledgement of ambiguity in the national identity of oneself and others would be a given in a multinational setting such as the Commission. However, an ethnographic study of the national identity of workers of the European Space Agency concludes that it was not a regular part of the "nationality talk" (Zabusky 2000: 186). It may be that since the translators are dealing daily with cultural differences on a very pragmatic level, they are perhaps also more aware of the complexities involved than other professional groups. This sensitivity may also explain the rather curious gap in humour: in the focus group discussions and my observation data, there is not one single instance of humour based on resorting to national stereotypes (with the possible exception of extract 17 which can be seen to play with a stereotyped image of Finns as an introvert and quiet people). It is worth noting that the very Finnish context of work does not seem to feed a stereotypical relation to the other nationalities in the "House of Translators" (cf. Bellier 2000; Zabusky 2000).

In many if not most instances of laughter, there is a sarcastic and ironic undertone as the participants create emotional distance to perceived ambiguities and discrepancies. These instances of irony and sarcasm might lead the observer to draw the conclusion that the participants are cynical and unmotivated. This kind of negativity may, however, be a normal feature of organizational talk in ambiguous situations (cf. Feldman 1991: 155). Irony can help in creating space for dealing with contradictory demands by allowing some distance to the official policies and normative expectations (Hatch 1997: 281). Similarly, Meyerson's study of social workers emphasizes the role of cynical humour as a legitimate expression of felt ambiguities. Cynicism, according to Meyerson, is a positive force: it enables the speakers to recognize the contradictory nature of their work lives without having to attempt to resolve the contradictions; it allows "unresolvables, irreconcilables, and untenables to remain unresolved" (1991: 141). Irony and sarcasm seem to have similar functions in the focus groups; it is not that the participants are attempting to laugh off some difficult issues. That is, by laughing or joking they are not just pretending that something is less serious than it is (Haakana 1999: 253). Instead, with the help of laughter they negotiate their level of personal involvement and maintain group cohesion in the face of potential disagreements.

5.5 Conclusions

The aim of this chapter was to analyze the way translators negotiate between their national and European identities, and how their profession affects their identities. As a subset of Commission officials, translators are visibly placed in a mediating position and forced by their profession to find ways of accommodating conflicting loyalties. Less immersed in the multinational "European" work setting and more explicitly connected to the national realities they have left behind than EU officials working in many other fields, translators negotiate the multiple affiliations of their nexus of identities in their daily work.

These identities are not fixed but blurred and constantly re-negotiable, and they defy binary logic. There is an innate ambivalence, where A and non-A can both be true at the same time: the translators are A-level officials, but at the same time they are a separate breed, different from A-level officials; within the Commission translators are a unified professional group, but their different educational backgrounds and previous work experiences shape their understandings of what this professional group is and should be; they are an integral part of the Commission, but separate from it; they see their task as serving the European citizens, but claim that they cannot take their readers into consideration. In managing this inherent ambivalence they resort to fostering group cohesion with devices such as group laughter and shared lunches.

6. Institutional Text Production

6.1 The social study of texts

It is fairly obvious that an ethnographic study of translation focuses on the socio-economic aspects of the profession and gives precedence to the participants' own voices. But I also want to stress that it is important not to overlook the social study of the translations themselves. An analysis of even a minute linguistic feature can give us clues to the social role of the translation and translators in either the source or the target community. In this chapter, the focus is on how texts – originals and translations – are both shaped by their social context and also participate in shaping that context.

Mapping the process

Linguistic case studies often concentrate on end products, the final documents, and contain little or no information on how the texts came to be as they are. Similarly, research on EU translation has dealt with final documents. This is understandable. Mapping the drafting process is not always feasible because, contrary to the published final documents, the intermediate versions are internal documents normally not available to the public. However, given the gradual drafting process and the intertwined drafting and translating processes, emphasis on final texts alone misses several essential factors. It has been argued that it would be a challenge to translation scholars to study "the actual text production-cum-translation process in order to find out how linguistic, cultural, legal, or ideological factors have an impact on the final versions of the texts" (Schäffner 2002: 105). In this chapter, I will take up this challenge and follow one text through the process of its multilingual formation.[1]

In addition to the final versions, my case consists of the unpublished preliminary drafts of a Communication (COM(2001)678) as well as the two Finnish translations. The selection criteria for the sample document were that (1) the original drafting language was English, (2) the text was translated into all official languages, and (3) the document went through a rewriting process (i.e., that there are several draft versions). A further criterion was that it is *not* a piece of actual legislation (multilingual legislation is a genre of its own, at least potentially different from other kinds of institutional translation). The case text was randomly selected, and without any prior analysis or even reading of its content. It was simply drawn from among those which met these external criteria and had successfully passed a 'normal' drafting process prior to the

---

[1] I wish to thank the DGT (then SdT) for giving me the opportunity to use the unpublished draft versions for research purposes.

time of data collection in 2002. This text is an average document, or even a conservative one, in that it has been rewritten three times. The number of versions is not limited in advance, and sometimes a document can be reworked in a dozen drafts or more. To increase effectiveness, and to reduce translation costs, it is standard procedure to limit the number of translated versions, especially in the 'lesser-used languages', to the very last one(s). In this case, the last two of the four versions were translated into Finnish. The case material includes the following versions:

In English: **In Finnish:**
ORI-00 (22 pages)
ORI-01 (30 pages)
ORI-02 (34 pages)   FI-TRA-02 (37)
ORI-03 (29 pages + notes, 5 p.) FI-TRA-03 (37)   (total: 194 pages)

A multi-stage comparative analysis was conducted of the four source text versions drafted in English and their two Finnish translations (other final versions – apart from Greek – were consulted for particular features but not subjected to an extensive analysis). The comparison and analysis included the following seven stages:

ORI-00 – ORI-01
ORI-01 – ORI-02
an independent reading of TRA-02
ORI-02 – TRA-02
ORI-02 – ORI-03
ORI-03 – TRA-03
TRA-02 – TRA-03

The aim of the comparative analysis was to uncover the institutional factors and interpersonal relations as they were manifested in the shifts of expression between the different versions. The analysis was textual and institutionally situated. First, I looked for evidence *in the texts*, not by observing verbalized thought-processes during writing or by participating in meetings where the draft versions were discussed (cf. Weiss and Wodak 2000). Second, I looked for explanations for the characteristics of the texts in their institutional context rather than in the mind of the writer or the translator. The aim was to combine close textual analysis with a social analysis of institutional production routines (Fairclough 1995: 9).

The analysis was strongly process-oriented. It is, however, necessary to distinguish it from how process-orientation is often understood in translation studies. In TS parlance, the word "process" is typically used with reference to the *mental* process involved in translation, to the investigation of the 'black box' inside the translator's head with the help of empirical methods such as think-aloud protocols and retrospection. Brian Mossop has proposed a different kind of process-orientedness: an analysis of translators' work-place procedures based on observation (2000). Both these research models will, no doubt, yield fascinating results when applied to any institutional framework. My approach to the process here is, however, different from them in two ways: first, it is neither psychological nor procedural but textual, and, second, it is not individual but collective and anonymous. The draft versions are not products of one master-mind (thus there is no one 'box' one could open) but the results of teamwork, commentaries, and co-drafting by anonymous writers, translators and revisers.

The different versions are like snapshots of a moving target. The process is in flux, and as such, it is an ephemeral object of study as its beginning and its end cannot be firmly fixed to any particular point in time. The origins of this particular text were established in numerous previous documents and undocumented discussions, and the final version of this communication was just a springboard for further action and new texts. To grasp the process, I fix my gaze on the snapshots, trusting that a detailed analysis of their features makes it possible to infer some aspects of the process. In the intermediate versions, in the products-in-process, the constant flow is at least momentarily stabilized.

Focus on shifts

The analysis of shifts is a traditional and well-known method in translation studies (here it is applied to the different source text versions as well). This method has its roots in the linguistic approaches of the 1950s and 1960s. In their comparative stylistic analysis of French and English, Vinay and Darbelnet (1958) developed a taxonomy of translation shifts, although they did not use that term. The term itself was coined by J.C. Catford (1965), who defined shifts as departures from *formal* correspondence between the source text and the target text. A recent textbook continues the linguistic tradition by defining translation shifts as "small linguistic changes occurring in translation of ST to TT" (Munday 2001: 55).

For the present purposes, however, the linguistic definition appears too formalistic and decontextualized. What I am looking for is not only the manifest linguistic expression of shifts but also their social causes and effects. For this purpose, the definition of shifts offered by Anton Popovič (1970: 79) is most suitable. According to Popovič, "[a]ll that appears new with respect to the original, or fails to appear where it might have been expected, may be interpreted as a shift". This definition encompasses not only linguistic and structural shifts, but also shifts that are textual, semantic, stylistic, ideological and functional.

This definition also emphasizes the interpretive aspects of shifts and focuses on reception: all that *appears* new, or is different from what was *expected*, may be *interpreted* as a shift. Shifts are thus not only a function of the relationship between the source text and the target text, but also a function of the relationship between the target text and the reader's (or researcher-reader's) expectations.

It is necessary to stress that 'shift' is not a synonym for a mistake (in fact, *correcting* mistakes in the original also results in shifts). Rather, one could claim that shifts are a universal feature of all translation (Toury 1995: 57): due to differences between languages, communicative situations, contexts and cultures, or in the last instance differences in reception, one can always discern shifts between source and target texts. Obviously, one can also discern shifts between the different versions of the source text – otherwise they would be identical. The notion of shift, however, entails an idea of subtlety. Although no clear division can be made, shifts may be less dramatic than changes, or less extensive. Shifts create subtle interpretive movements, differences of tone and emphasis between the versions.[2] In my analysis, I did not classify the shifts according to their size: for practical reasons, small nuances and drastic omissions were treated equally.

Shifts imply choices (conscious or not); an analysis of shifts can thus be aligned with the view of texts as "networks of systems of options which are selected amongst in the production of texts" (Fairclough 1995: 5; see also Halliday 1985). If each semantic choice has its own meaning potential, each shift of expression also results in shifting the meaning potential. In an institution such as the European Commission that aims to be efficient, giving up a previous formulation and providing a new one can be interpreted as a strong and purposeful choice that cannot be justified by chance or idiosyncratic preferences (especially when we take into account the replication of the effort for all languages in translation). These changes can thus reveal significant processes of actualizing and emphasizing particular meanings, and of subduing and hiding others.

On the other hand, shifts are not always intentional, and some shifts are caused by differences between language systems and textual conventions. For that reason shifts have been traditionally divided into two categories: obligatory and optional (Vinay and Darbelnet 1958). For some purposes, this difference

---

[2] The problem of *tertium comparationis* and the related issue of equivalence are in-built in the notion of translation shifts: defining a particular rendering as a shift assumes a 'non-shifting' *tertium comparationis*, and selecting shifts for closed analysis implies that other parts of the translation are similar to or equivalent with the source text. The problem of similarity versus difference is a core question of translation, and has been debated for centuries (see Koskinen 2001). For practical reasons, I will side-step the issue here. (See Chesterman 1998: 29-36; Toury 1995: 85).

between obligatory and optional shifts may be crucial (Blum-Kulka 1986/2000: 312). Within the framework provided by Popovič's definition, assessing the degree of intentionality and voluntariness is, nevertheless, of secondary value. Defining shifts on the basis of expectedness, and the parallel phenomenon of the non-occurrence of shifts where they may be expected, emphasize aspects related to reception rather than production: it becomes more relevant to ponder what kinds of shifts take place and how they affect the outcome than to categorize the degree of voluntariness in translator strategies. An analysis of the shifts that take place during the process of drafting the original and its Finnish translation can help to explain how EU documents became the way they are, and perhaps also offer some explanations as to why they are so often felt to fail in communicating the European message to citizens. The occurrence of shifts, or, as may be, the non-occurrence of shifts, in the translated versions can also further illuminate to the role and task of the translators.

Interpersonal shifts

The strong taxonomic tradition in the study of translation shifts poses problems for the present analysis. Ever since Catford as well as Vinay and Darbelnet published their views, shifts seem to have inspired scholars to develop classifications of great detail and complexity. Kitty van Leuven-Zwart's model (1990) of different micro- and macrostructural shifts is the most extensive to date (see also Chesterman 1997). With its attention to the Hallidayan interpersonal, ideational and textual metafunctions, the Leuven-Zwart model transcends the purely linguistic level and introduces social considerations. In practice, however, the sheer volume of shifts in my data called for a simplified taxonomy: all versions have been analyzed in their entirety, and the various comparisons resulted in more than 400 pages of text to be subjected to comparative analysis. There is hardly a page without shifts, and many pages get completely revamped in new versions. As a result, a detailed classification proved a hopeless task. To keep track of the overall picture, I first created my own simplified system of classification: additions/omissions, change of location within the text, lexical changes (semantic/prosody/tenor) and grammatical/structural changes. Even within this simple taxonomy, quantification was complicated. The drafted versions in the original language, in particular, posed problems: If an entire page is totally rewritten, is it to be counted as one huge shift or one hundred? If an entirely new appendix is added, is this one addition or many?

After the first rough analysis, I focused on those recurrent features which appeared most significant from the point of view of institutional cultures and identifications that are under study here. In the present analysis, two kinds of shifts have received particular attention: first, those which might illuminate aspects of the entire process and the role of translators in it (that is, issues of the organizational role and status of the translators) and, second, those which have a bearing on the interpersonal function of the text. These interpersonal shifts in aspects such as hedges, boosters, directives, self-mention and ingroup-outgroup classifications can be studied to assess how this particular text creates and negotiates distances and affinities (see Hyland 2005). According to Halliday's systemic-functional model, all languages are organized around two 'metafunctions': the ideational (reflecting the environment) and the interpersonal (relating to others); the third, textual metafunction "breaths relevance" into the other two (1985: xiii). Focusing on interpersonal shifts, this study works in parallel with two recent contributions to the study of translations produced in institutional settings from the point of view of ideational shifts. María Calzada Pérez (2001) and Ian Mason (2003) have both focused on transitivity shifts, and transitivity is typically classified as belonging to the ideational metafunction of texts (Mason 2003: 176; see also Blum-Kulka 1986/2000 for an analysis of textual shifts).

In texts, the ideational, the interpersonal and the textual meet and mingle (for example, propositional content also reflects the writer's ideas of the knowledge shared by the intended readers), and too strict a division is not advisable. But the present emphasis is on the textual manifestations of the nexus of relations, that is, on the interpersonal aspects. Particular attention will be placed on the roles assigned to the institutional writer and the reader(s) of the text in the various drafts. In practice, this is accomplished by analyzing how the Commission as the institutional writer presents itself, and how it addresses the readers, how the writer relates to other actors and to the ideational content of the text, and what the writer expects from other actors. For example, I will study the writer's self-references, his or her ways of speaking about and to the addressees (e.g., the use of modal verbs and markers of evaluation, that is, ways of expressing attitudes towards what is said).

Calzada Pérez's and Mason's work on transitivity shifts provided very useful parallel studies, and will be referred to below. There is, however, a significant difference between their research and the present endeavour that needs to be mentioned here. Their analysis of transitivity shifts is in both cases motivated by an attempt to test whether one can discern a particular policy of translation or translational culture, to reveal the "underlying attitudes towards text and translating" (Mason 2003: 176). Calzada Pérez takes my hypothesis of an EU culture as her starting point – and comes to refute my claim of its existence – but I think we see the question of culture somewhat differently. Similar to Mason, she seems to equate EU culture with a guiding principle of EU translation (2001: 212). For me, it originally referred to the specific reality the translators translate from, independently of selected translation strategies (for a more detailed discussion of the debate, see Koskinen 2004).

This difference prevails here: while my research still revolves around the question of EU culture, and does so from the point of view of translators, and while it can in that sense be seen as a study of translational culture, I wish to maintain an analytic difference between translation strategies and translation cultures.[3]

This study does not include a quantifiable analysis of a computerized corpus. Instead, this chapter presents the results of a far more traditional and manual qualitative analysis of one case.[4] Like Sari Eskola, a Finnish corpus researcher, I feel that it is also valuable to immerse oneself in the text, to dwell on it in order to get an overall feeling of its salient qualities (see Eskola 2002: 267-268). This is advantageous in assessing both the relative weight and importance of different shifts and the overall impact of several kinds of shifts. Concatenating shifts may shift the entire discourse (Mason 2003: 184), and these effects may be easier to detect in close reading. By contrast, corpus study detaches the researcher from the data and fragments the findings. This is not to be interpreted as a value judgement on my part: the objectifying power of corpus study, and the possibility of dealing with huge amounts of data, can be and has already been a valuable asset in translation studies. It is rather a question of researcher personalities and division of labour: I feel more confident and competent in a small-scale study; someone else with different preferences can perhaps benefit from my findings in designing a corpus study of EU texts.

This chapter presents the findings of a multi-stage comparative analysis. Section 6.2 presents the different stages of the *drafting* process of the original document. This will then bring us to the *translation* process in section 6.3. Section 6.4 discusses one feature, modality, and more specifically the use of the conditional, in a detailed analysis. Section 6.5 concludes the discussion.

6.2 Drafting process

It is quite common in many institutional settings to have 'document chains' in the sense that each document is anticipated for (or regulated) in previous documents, and it in turn paves the way to new documents taking the issue further. The case document, *Communication from the Commission. Making a European Area of Lifelong Learning a Reality* (COM (2001) 678), is an illustrative example of this

---

[3] Another potential difference may be the use of in-house rather than freelance texts. Neither Calzada Pérez nor Mason gives explicit information on whether their data had been translated by in-house translators or freelancers, but it is a plausible assumption that the European Parliament data might have been outsourced. This, of course, would have a bearing on the translators' socialization to an in-house translation culture.

[4] My data were tentatively also analyzed with corpus tools, but the sample proved too small to be effective for my present purposes. I wish to thank Hanna Westerlund for her assistance in this experiment.

intertextuality. This is because the document is based on numerous prior state-ments and action programmes such as the European Year of Lifelong Learning in 1996 and the Lisbon strategy of the year 2000 (the by now infamous aim to become the most competitive and dynamic knowledge-based society in the world). At the Feira European Council in June 2000, the Commission and the member states were explicitly called upon to define a strategy of lifelong learn-ing. This task was taken up by the commissioners responsible for education and employment. The result was that they issued a proposal that initiated the drafting process of the communication which was then revised and translated and then issued in eleven official languages in November 2001.

The communication is also linked to *future* documents. First, it was part of the Commission's contribution to the March 2002 European Council. Second, it includes an in-built follow-up system in that the Commission promised to submit a progress report to the European Council and the European Parliament. Third, it contains a number of proposals for future action such as partnerships and the sharing of best practice, tax incentives, information and guidance services and research. All these are largely actualized with the help of various documents. The communication also suggests new kinds of documents to be developed (a portfolio system based on the European CV, European training diplomas and certificates, and a European label).

The intertextual chain is not limited to written documents. Prior to the actual drafting, an extensive Europe-wide consultation process was undertaken, which in turn was laid out in the then recent White Paper on European Governance (2001) calling for more democratic and participatory working methods. This consultation process culminated in a large conference with representatives of civil society in Brussels in September 2001. The case document, in other words, reflects the 'participatory turn' of the EU (see Chapter 4) in practical terms: it has been preceded by a new procedure, where new efforts have been taken to enhance consultation ('participation via consultation' being the Com-mission's interpretation of participatory processes; see Abels 2002: 12). As a result, this document offers a possibility for empirically assessing whether the new policy line is also manifest in textual evidence. It has been argued that the new emphasis on citizens and dialogue may be merely tokenism or an at-tempt to cover up the democratic deficit (see Abels 2002; Bora and Hausendorf 2006). An analysis of the case document may provide some evidence either for or against these claims. This may also shed some light on the question of whether the translators, who are not addressed in the policy papers and whose contribution is not singled out as being relevant to the new, participatory aims (see Chapter 4), still try to find pragmatic strategies to support it.

The political process thus creates another process level above others. Similar to the concept of context, the exact scope of which is hardly possible to define, the concept of process can be employed on different levels. On the most intimate level is the mental process of both drafting and translating a text (cf. TAPs). Another level is composed of the practical work-place processes involved in the production of each version (cf. Mossop 2000). Further up, there is the entire drafting process whereby the preliminary drafts are revised, retranslated and reworked until the final document is agreed on. This drafting process is the process under study here. Over and above it, there are the (never-ending) political and practical processes that tie the various documents together. The texts bear traces of each of these processes.

In the following, I will summarize the findings relating to the shifts that take place between the four versions of the original (ORI00 – ORI03). At each phase, a multitude of shifts take place. This overview focuses on those characteristics relevant to studying textual manifestation of the nexus of relations and cultural identifications.

Political redrafting (ORI-00 → ORI-01)

The most immediately recognizable difference between the first and second drafts of the original version is their length. The ORI-00 version of the report is 22 pages long whereas the ORI-01 is 30 pages (annexes were not included in the analysis). The additions thus add up to eight pages. Out of these, however, four pages are explained by the predominately technical fact that the first version did not yet include the Executive Summary that is a standard part of each communication and was only drafted for the second version. Extensive background information has also been added to the introduction. However, few changes have been made to the main points and proposed concrete actions, as most of the additions, the few omissions and the shifting expressions take place in the explanatory parts and background information around these main points.

One typical reason for these additions is the need to add new information (for example, footnotes increase from 34 to 44), and specifications or references to assist the reader (such as "see section 3.6"). Several additions are best described as instances of explicitation. For example:

> formulated according to *the broad definition, objectives* and principles of lifelong learning (ORI-00) → formulated according to *the four objectives of active citizenship, personal fulfilment, employablility and social inclusion,* as well as the principles of lifelong learning (ORI-01) (italics added)

> in the implementation of lifelong learning (ORI-00) → in *facilitating access* to learning, and in *motivating* potential learners (ORI-01) (italics in the original)

Several additions consist of buzz words of contemporary education policy. These reinforce a particular ideology of learning, bringing the learner to the forefront. The additions include concepts such as "learners' individual pathways", "individual pathways of learning", "learner-centred approach", and "to foster a culture of learning" (ORI-01). A related set of recurring additions increases the emphasis on people, reflecting the contemporary EU policy of European citizenship. For example: "active citizenship", "promoting real active citizenship", and "as close to the citizens as possible" (ORI-01).

Together, these two sets of additions emphasize the role of individual learners and active citizens, that is, the 'normal' people outside the spheres of the decision makers and civil servants. This emphasis is crystallized at the very beginning of the document: "People are at the heart of this communication". Contrasting the additions with the main set of omissions, however, reveals a contradictory picture that makes the opening sentence sound hollow. To a great extent, the omissions follow the pattern of systematically playing down the role of the consultation process which preceded the communication and then of pushing forward the active role of the Commission. Omissions include such statements as "many contributions suggested", "feedback emphasized", "many respondents advocated", "respondents said", "the feedback also identified", and "the content rooted on this feedback" (ORI-00).

This systematic pattern of pushing the Commission to the forefront cuts across other categories of shifts as well. For instance, an innocuous-looking shift of tense results in a different view of who the active partner is:

> were called for [in the feedback] (ORI-00) → is called for [in this Commission communication] (ORI-01)
> was particularly stressed [in the feedback] (ORI-00) → is particularly relevant [according to the European Commission-cum-writer] (ORI-01)

There are, in other words, two contradictory processes in the text: bringing added emphasis on the present policy lines, the second version advocates the importance of learners and people. Several shifts also add to the readability of the text, helping the reader by added information, guidance and explicitation. This reader-friendly and learner-centred promotion of active citizenship, however, is undermined by the omissions, which create exactly the opposite effect: the voice of the "over 12.000 citizens [who] contributed to the consultation" is effectively muted, and the Commission elbows itself to the forefront.

Institutional redrafting (ORI-01 → ORI-02)

The second round of drafting follows a different logic. The same broad categories of addition, omission, linguistic and semantic changes exist, but within them, the shifts serve functions that are different from those of the previous draft.

Again, the text grows longer (30 pages → 34 pages). Apart from a drastic cut of all the overall conclusions in the last chapter (three paragraphs) and two of the four annexes, omissions are few and largely minor. Interestingly, several of the omissions concern features that were purposefully added in the previous draft (e.g., the elimination of "work in partnership"). Added material consists of new references, often acronyms, to other documents and EU institutions and to the previous work done in the Commission (e.g., ESF, The European Investment Bank, EQUAL, Skills and Mobility Action Plan). This tendency is visible both within the main text and in the drastic (further) increase in the number of footnotes from 44 to 74. In other words, the institutional framework of the document is demarcated more clearly.

The overall focus of the second round of rewriting is on this institutional framework and jurisdiction, but there are also two shifts with ideological overtones. First, references to research issues are added, in particular to the European research area. Second, all references to "skills" are equally sys-tematically omitted (apart from the Skills and Mobility Action Plan which is a fixed name). In addition to the total omissions, "skills" is rephrased as "competences" or "knowledge". This shifting back and forth between additions and omissions in subsequent versions indicates some internal controversies relating to the policy lines.

The version ORI-02 also establishes more explicitly the legal basis, and the limits of the Commission mandate. There are also numerous instances of added hedging or more careful formulations, delimiting the extent to which commitment is expressed:

> will be fully integrated into (ORI-01) → will be taken into account in (ORI-02)
> will be crucial in (ORI-01) → will provide new opportunities for (ORI-02)
> will also ensure (ORI-01) → will help to ensure (ORI-02)
> the Commission will (ORI-01) → this work will (ORI-02)

The added institutionalization of the style is further strengthened by semantic shifts leading to more complicated phrases and added fuzziness. For example:

> lays the ground (ORI-01) → contributes to the establishment (ORI-02)
> work together (ORI-01) → collaborate (ORI-02)
> gender equality (ORI-01) → gender mainstreaming (ORI-02)
> simplification of directives (ORI-01) → a more uniform, transparent and flexible regime (ORI-02)
> job opportunities (ORI-01) → labour market systems (ORI-02)

On the other hand, there are also some examples of attempted 'normalization' in shifts:

> human resources (ORI-01) → learners at all ages (ORI-02)
> to benchmark (ORI-01) → to measure (ORI-02)

Many of the shifts in the ORI-02 are related to readability. The most extensive addition towards this aim is that each subchapter of this version opens with a short summary of the main points. In addition to the structural changes in the representation format and order (e.g., the use of bullets), there are also several shifts which make the intended meaning more explicit, for example by spelling out deictic expressions:

> they (ORI-01) → the priorities (ORI-02)
> this (ORI-01) → the development of indicators (ORI-02)
> on this subject (ORI-01) → on lifelong learning (ORI-02)

Reframing the document (ORI-02 → ORI-03)

In the final redrafting stage, the alterations take place almost exclusively in the framework parts of the document: in the executive summary, the introduction and the summary. The actual content of the proposed actions remains largely untouched, give or take a few additions. In fact, only one section (on indicators) is extensively rewritten. The framework, then, is reworked to the extent that it becomes close to impossible to track down the individual shifts: in the executive summary, for example, one third of the previous material is omitted entirely. Searching for recurrent patterns in omitted and added material reveals that the explicit emphasis reflecting value judgements tends to be omitted. For instance, omitted sections include the following (italics added):

> Lifelong learning *revolutionises* thinking about schools and other institutions of learning [. . .] Education and training systems *simply must be transformed* to accommodate this new approach. Furthermore, *this approach must provide new opportunities* for citizens to live, work and learn in Member States other than their own. (ORI-02)

> [Gaining insight] *is fundamental to* the learner-centred approach. (ORI-02)

> Targeting support at groups at risk of exclusion is also *a key consideration* and innovative ways of delivering learning are *advocated*. Promoting local learning centres is seen *as a particularly useful way of removing barriers* to learning. (ORI-02)

These and numerous other similar omissions in the four-page summary result in an overall flattening effect after which the reader is given little help in assessing the writers' priorities and in differentiating between 'key considerations' and secondary actions. For a document such as this, explicitly sending a plea for action, this development is unfortunate. Instead of sending a message that something 'simply must' be achieved, the final version leaves it to the readers to find that excitement and persistence for themselves.

Additions then are often used for added information and clarification, but there are also systematic additions of political keywords ("science and technology", "research", "tolerance" and "democratic values"). In brief, in each draft version there are some favourite buzz words sprinkled generously throughout the document.

The final version also continues other earlier processes. Here again some attempt is made to improve readability (deictic expressions and sentence structures), but EU jargon and officialese also increase (e.g., training plan (ORI-02) → competence development plan (ORI-03)). The effacement of the consultation process also continues, and the Commission is foregrounded while the role of other institutional actors is played down. For example:

> The *consultation feedback identified* a number of core elements of any successful approach and these are presented as the building blocks of coherent and comprehensive strategies. (ORI-02) → The building blocks of [coherent and comprehensive] strategies *are set out here* to assist Member States and actors at all levels. (ORI-03) (italics added)

> the European Council then invited (ORI-02) → the Commission then adopted . . . on the invitation of the European Council (ORI-03)

> Research undertaken in the Member States, the OECD and by groups of experts (ORI-02) → current research (ORI-03)

Drafting process: summary

An analysis of the shifts that take place between the four different versions of the communication reveals two basic tendencies. First, there is a clear attempt towards clarification and added readability. I rather expected to find some textual deterioration (e.g., reduced coherence) or fragmentation caused by the extensive changes, omissions and additions, but there is very little evidence of that. Instead, many shifts are related to explicitation, indicating a concern for readability. Explicitation has been listed as one potential translation universal, i.e., as a likely feature of all translations, regardless of their context and content (Blum-Kulka 1986/2000: 300). This case seems to suggest that explicitation might in fact be a universal of *all* kinds of rewriting, with or without language change. In other words, this data supports the hypothesis made by Sandra Halverson (2003) that translation universals may not be translation-specific but rather related to more general cognitive processes. Many characteristics of translation may be explained by its metalinguistic nature. It may thus not come as a surprise that translation has features in common with other kinds of metalinguistic activities. Halverson uses second language acquisition as the basis of her comparison; it might be fruitful to use revision practices as a similarly parallel case.

Attempts to enhance readability in my case document, however, are thwarted by the second tendency, that of the institution pushing itself to the forefront. This tendency manifests itself in many ways: in the effacement of the consultation process and other actors, in the choice of more complicated and bureaucratic expressions, in drawing the limits of the Commission man-date, and in the generous application of the favourite buzz words. The case indeed shows how the institution rewrites the document to meet its interests and needs. The alienation effect of all this institutionalization outweighs the attempts towards reader-friendliness. The problem of balancing the institutional discourses with the newly enforced emphasis on readability is epitomized in one of the appendices, which consists of a glossary of the key terms used in the communication. The list includes terms and coinages such as "active citizenship", "digital divide", "European governance", "formal, informal and non-formal learning" and "lifewide learning" [sic]. This glossary is of obvious assistance to uninitiated readers not familiar with the vogue of education policy and EU jargon, but the sheer existence of the glossary pinpoints the problem: if the communication cannot be understood without the help of a four-page glossary, its language is probably too specialized to begin with.

The two mutually counter-productive sub-processes within the drafting proc-ess are, in other words, those of clarification and institutionalization. It is therefore striking that neither one appears to be systematic. In none of the versions do shifts focus on improving the textual qualities of the document to substantially improve its readability. Likewise, shifts affecting the institutional and political framework are made on the surface level, e.g., in the form of slogans and catch words, and the actual content of the document remains unchanged.

6.3 Translation process

Above we followed the gradual gestation of the original text. This long and winding process of drafting has been identified as one major obstacle for translation:

> What makes these texts difficult to process is their tortuous progress, involving several different services and several different political

levels, generating several successive versions and repeated translation of nuances and details whose point is often obscure. (Wagner et al. 2002: 48)

An overview of the drafting process of this case document revealed a surprisingly unified picture. Although the texts pass different political levels (with their favourite buzz words), the shifts taking place in each successive version mainly re-enforce the two processes of clarification and institutionalization begun at earlier versions. But how does translation fit into this picture? Does it continue along the same lines, or does it introduce new kinds of shifts? And will the need for repeated translation of 'obscure nuances' lead to a loss of coherence?

Communicating in Finnish (independent reading of TRA-02)

The first stage of my analysis of the Finnish translation involved reading it on its own, without any source text comparison, to see how it functions as a text in its own right. My first encounter with the first version written in my native language took place only after I had already read and analyzed three English versions. I was thus already well acquainted with the subject matter. Still, my first reaction was that the text was difficult. After reading the summary I wrote in my notes: "How come this is so difficult? I cannot make any sense of this!". An equally strong observation, however, was that the translation was in many ways successful in that it avoided many of the pitfalls that I remembered well from the past and that were also identified in an earlier critical evaluation of Finnish translations in the EU (Karvonen 1996). For example, the grammar and syntax of this version were not un-Finnish (apart from what appeared to be an excessive number of conditional forms, which will be discussed in more detail later), and the text style was not clumsy. The case text thus seemed to be a good translation that was difficult to understand. A major task of my analysis, then, was to find out the causes for this perceived difficulty. Some explanations were easy to find. Recurrent features of the difficult passages were, for example, long and winding noun phrases, with long chains of genitive modifiers, and these reduced their readability. Chains of modifiers in left-branching phrases (i.e., genitives preceding the head noun) make the overall style heavy, and in the worst cases these phrases were close to indecipherable. In the following examples, the noun phrases are put in square brackets (the first, and the shortest, example is analyzed in more detail) and the head nouns are marked with italics. The title of the document, with its embedded chains of modifiers, sets the tone:

[[Eurooppalaisen [elinikäisen oppimisen] alueen] *toteuttaminen]*
gloss: European+GEN lifelong+GEN learning+GEN area+GEN
realization
(Orig. Making the European *Area* of Lifelong Learning a Reality)

Many of the chains of modifiers are quite extensive. The following two sentences both contain a noun phrase with nine different modifiers, and the sentences mainly consist of noun phrases and the verb:

[Indikaattoreiden *kehittämistä*] valvotaan periaatteessa [koulujärjes- telmien konkreettisia tulevaisuuden tavoitteita koskevaa selvitystä seuraamaan perustetun asiantuntijaryhmien *verkoston*] avulla.
(Orig. [This *development*] will, in principle, be overseen through [the *network* of expert groups] formed to follow up the [*Report* on the Concrete Objectives of Education and Training Systems].)

[Lissabonin Eurooppa-neuvostossa esitetyn tietoon perustuvan tavoitteen [sic] luomista koskevan tavoitteen *saavuttamiseksi*] [euroop- palaisen elinikäisen oppimisen *alueen*] on oltava tiiviisti yhteydessä [eurooppalaiseen tutkimus*alueeseen*].
(Orig. In particular, in order to achieve [the Lisbon *aim* of a knowl- edge-based society], [the European *area* of lifelong learning] should be closely linked with [the European Research *Area*].)

These examples show that the number of modifiers largely originates in the source text, but whereas the English text alternates between pre- and postmodifiers, and adds rhythm and emphasis to the text with the help of sen- tential adverbs and commas ("in particular", "in principle"), the Finnish opts exclusively for premodifiers and has a tendency towards nominalized head nouns (on similar tendencies in Danish EU translations, see Trosborg 1997). These long chains of modifiers have been identified as a typical feature of Finnish official texts. Noun phrases are seen as a means of standardizing the ideational contents; relations, actors and processes are all expressed by a chain of genitive attributes. As a result, speculations, presuppositions and contested views all appear to be naturalized (Heikkinen et al. 2000: 53-56).

Other features in this text are the extensive use of the passive voice, abstract style, neologisms, fixed phrases and terms (such as "elinikäinen oppiminen" for "lifelong learning") as well as specialized bureaucratic vocabulary in the Finnish translation. All in all, this translation is similar in many ways to the standard official documents produced daily by the various national authorities in Finland (for an overview of Finnish official language, see Heikkinen et al. 2000). This case document thus seems to be a counterexample to my previous claim, based on my own experiences during the early years of Finnish mem- bership, that Finnish EU translations sound strange and peculiar because of their foreignizing 'overdomestication' strategy (Koskinen 2000ab; cf. Calzada Pérez 2001). This translation attests to a normalization of translation routines in that the text seems to suffer from difficulties that are likewise familiar in many nationally produced official texts.

Continued institutionalization (ORI-02→TRA-02)

The second stage of analysis, a comparative reading of the original version
(ORI-02) and its Finnish translation, shed more light on the question of
readability, but it also made the picture more complex. Similar to the draft
versions of the original, this translation introduces numerous shifts towards
added readability: complex sentence structures are simplified, long sentences
are cut into two, deictic expressions and references to EU events and institutions are made more explicit and acronyms are spelled out. So, even though
this translation aims at helping the reader out, my reading experience was
one of difficulty. Comparative analysis of the source and target texts reveals a
number of recurrent shifts and these add to the problems of readability. Three
groups of shifts seem particularly relevant in this respect: bureaucratization
of the style, omission of the words marking an evaluation or appraisal, and
loss of metaphors.

The Finnish translation 'normalizes' the language of the original towards
the style of typical official texts (cf. above). The original, of course, is already
a representative of what the English tend to call Euro-jargon, but the Finnish translation takes this trait one step further. Wordings that are 'normal' or
even colloquial English tend to get officialized in the Finnish translation.[5]
For example:

> to be (ORI-02) → perustaa alue [to establish an area] (TRA-02)
> to be (ORI-02) → alueen luominen [the creation of an area] (TRA-02)
> – some way off . . . (an 'afterthought' separated by a dash) (ORI-02)
> → Tulos ei siis vastaa . . . [The result does not in other words cor-
> respond . . .] (a separate sentence) (TRA-02)
> 'tuning' project (ORI-02) → yhdenmukaistamishanke [coordination
> project] (TRA-02)

There is also an unexpectedly high number of additions and omissions
in this translation. These additions mainly consist of added information and
repetition to help the reader. One interesting set of additions concerns the word
"skills", which had carefully been deleted from the original version during the
drafting process. The translator, who only enters the scene in the third version
of the source text, has no knowledge of these prior events. What happens is that
the "skills" returns to the translation. On two separate occasions, this translator
interprets "knowledge and competences" in its more familiar EU collocation
of "knowledge, skills and competences", and adds the Finnish translation of

---

[5] There are, however, also some examples of a movement in the opposite direction, for
example: interface (ORI-02) → kohtaaminen [meeting] (TRA-02).

"skills". The practice of delaying translation until the last versions undoubtedly improves efficiency, but the drawback is that the translator is then unaware of previous decisions such as this (some additions made in the ORI-02 were also omitted, attesting to the same problem).

Whereas the additions made during the translation process can be seen as assisting the reader, the more numerous omissions are more dubious in character. Some are fairly unimportant reductions caused by simplified sentence structures and expressions, but my overall impression is that the strategy of simplification and clarified language actually backfires. As a consequence, I find the frequent omission of different markers of evaluation, that is, indications of attitudes in the text, particularly problematic. If you take out words such as "potential" [in: potential benefits], "just" [the proportion was just 60.3%], "genuinely" [making learning genuinely available for all], "tend to" [measures tend to be piecemeal → are], "much" [much more open], "more actively" [promote more actively], "risk" [risk limiting → limit], "particularly", "in particular", and "as far as possible", the reader loses the cues for interpreting the writer's attitude and degree of engagement towards the propositions (see also J.R. Martin 1997 on 'appraisal'). It would appear that this simplified propositional structure with less interpersonal input fails to make the text easier and clearer and instead succeeds in making it *more difficult* to comprehend. This simplification strategy resembles the 'normalization' and 'localization' processes that Calzada Pérez (2001: 233) found in her corpus of European Parliament speeches, prompting her to pose the question of whether the translators are contributing to creating a Europe of the lowest common denominator (cf. Trosborg 1997).

The simplification strategy also applies to metaphors. The original version employs several metaphors. The Finnish translation has a demonstrated tendency to opt for less metaphoric solutions. For example:

> building blocks (ORI-02) → perustekijät [basic factors] (TRA-02)
> the next step is . . . (ORI-02) → seuraavan perustekijän mukaan tarkoituksena on [according to the next basic factor the intention is. . .] (TRA-02)
> has a key role to play (ORI-02) → vaikuttavat merkittävästi [have a significant impact] (TRA-02)
> key messages (ORI-02) → keskeiset aiheet [central themes] (TRA-02)
> powerful engine (ORI-02) → merkittävä vaikutus [significant impact] (TRA-02)
> vital cornerstones (ORI-02) → perusta [foundation] (TRA-02)

In order to see whether shifts away from metaphoric language are a general trend among other language versions as well, I checked the chosen translation strategies for three focal metaphoric expressions in all languages (except Greek). The three source text metaphors selected for this analysis were those of 'the heart', 'the key' and 'the building blocks'. In their relevant co-text, they appear as follows:

Heart: People are at the heart of this communication. (ORI-03)
Key: Yet people, their knowledge and competences are the key to Europe's future. (ORI-03)
Building blocks: This section presents the building blocks for developing and implementing such strategies. (ORI-03)

	Heart	Key	building blocks
DA	det centrale	Nøglen	byggesten
DE	im Zentrum	der Schlüssel	'Bausteine'
ES	el núcleo	la clave	los componentes
FR	au centre	dépend des citoyens	les composantes essentielles
IT	al centro	dipende	le componenti essenziali
NL	gaat over mensen	de sleutel	bouwstenen
POR	no cerne	a chave	módulos constitutivos
SV	i centrum	nyckeln	byggelementen
FI	etusijalla [in a priority position]	kansalaisilla on merkittävä vaikutus [citizens have a significant impact]	perustekijät [basic factors]

Table 6.1: Translation of metaphoric expressions

As can be seen from Table 6.1, there is no standard system of translating metaphor by metaphor, nor is there a pattern of always translating metaphor by non-metaphor. None of the versions renders all three with an image similar to that of the original, and the heart, in particular, proves a touchstone: none of the other language versions resorts to similar warm-hearted expressions, and while the images of the centre or the nucleus can also be seen as metaphoric, their connotations are quite different from that of the heart which the English language, quite luckily, can pick up from its standard repertoire to serve the new emphasis on citizens. Nevertheless, many versions retain the concrete images of the key or the building blocks (or both).

According to Gideon Toury (1995: 84), one can assume that the reduced use of metaphors in target texts is motivated by target norms. This case would indicate that the Finnish norms of official language are less favourable to

metaphoric expressions than many other EU languages. Other possible explanations can be found in studies of journalistic translation. Maria Sidiropoulou
(2004: 80-81) suggests that in addition to normative constraints, translators
(in the Greek press; see Vuorinen 1996: 218 for similar findings in the Finnish press) might be deliberately minimizing the amount of effort required to
produce a translation or favouring accuracy over appropriateness. All three
sound plausible here, too. Be that as it may, for my present purposes it is more
interesting to ponder how this demetaphorization strategy affects the readers'
relation to the text. The loss of metaphoric language produces the same effect
as the omission of evaluative markers and the officialization of style: an overall
monotonizing of the text, making it more tiresome to read and, consequently,
harder to comprehend.

Analysis of shifts vs. independent reading

A further comparison of the results of the independent reading of the translation with those of the comparative analysis of the ORI-02 and the TRA-02
also yielded some interesting findings. This analysis showed that some heavy
structures were the result of information added for the benefit of the reader, but
also that some seemingly fluent renderings were the result of omissions, over-
simplification or blatant mistranslations. In the following I will concentrate
on two recurrent features: Finnish translation's resistance to buzz words, and
mistranslations. The translation of the modal verb "should" will be discussed
in a separate subsection (6.4) below.

As we saw in the analysis of the original versions, liberal amounts of buzz
words (of both EU and education policy) had been added to the document
during the various stages of the drafting process. I had found the neologisms
related to the learner-centred approach quite annoying in the translation (at
least to me). But in comparison it turned out that the Finnish version was in
fact far more traditional than the English. In the educational ideology the communication is based on, schools have become "learning providers"; teachers
do not teach – they are described as "delivering learning", or even "bringing
learning to the learner" in the "learning communities" situated in "learning
cities". To an extent, the Finnish version follows suit, but it also resorts to
more traditional expressions. For example:

> learning opportunities (ORI-02) → koulutus [education]; opiskelumah-
> dollisuudet [possibilities for study] (TRA-02)
> deliver learning (ORI-02) → tarjota koulutusta [to offer education]
> (TRA-02)

This resistance in the Finnish translation to markers of the educational
ideology promoted in the communication posits an interesting question: is

there, as a result, a difference between the English and the Finnish version in terms of policy line, and are the English readers of the communication then responding to a different proposal from the Finns? Or is it that the same educational ideology is linguistically expressed with more traditional terms in Finnish?

The resistance poses questions concerning the ideational content of the text, but the translation also continues the central interpersonal processes already started during the drafting of the original. In addition to the mutually contradictory processes of bureaucratization and added readability, this translation also contributes to the effacement of the consultation and the naturalization of the Commission viewpoints, as does the TRA-03 (cf. a contrastive finding in English EP translations in Calzada Pérez 2001):

> given the importance *attributed to* non-formal and informal learning (in consultation) (ORI-02) → koska epävirallisen ja arkioppimisen merkitys on niin suuri [because the importance of non-formal and informal learning *is* so great] (says the Commission here) (TRA-02) (italics added)

> the consultation stressed (ORI-03) → kuulemisen yhteydessä tähdennettiin [in connection with the consultation it was stressed] (TRA-03) (active to passive voice)

One feature that came up in the comparison of the ORI-02 and the TRA-02 was the number of various kinds of mistranslations. Some of them were pure slips, perhaps caused by a lack of time, such as the translation of "NGOs" as "työmarkkinaosapuolet" [social partners]. Others were misunderstandings which could have been caused by an unfamiliarity with the field, such as "competence forecasting activity" → "aktiivisuustasoa ennakoiva osaaminen" [competence that forecasts activity] instead of "osaamistarpeiden ennakoiminen" [activity of forecasting competence needs]. Some mistakes were more unfortunate. The repeated translation of "community" as "kunta" [municipality], for example, effectively confused matters on numerous occasions: "community education projects" became education projects organized by the municipal authorities; "local community organizations" become "paikalliset kuntajärjestöt" [local municipal organizations]. The rendering of "community learning provision" (as an example of non-formal learning) as "kunnissa tarjottava oppiminen" [learning provided by municipalities] is particularly confusing since Finland has few private schools, and the municipalities are the main providers of *formal* education.

I was surprised to find that the translation contained so many omissions and mistranslations that had a significant impact on content. Out of the some 40 (depending on how the recurrent mistranslations are counted) more serious errors, fifteen had caught my attention in one way or another during the independent reading (i.e., I had realized that there was some incoherence or confusion in the text); 25 had seemed fine to me. That is, an unsuspecting reader could not tell there was something missing or wrong. The high number of mistranslations indicates lack of time and also limited revision. One needs to remember, however, that TRA-02 was a draft translation, and the adoption of less than optimal solutions is thus not a major issue. It is more important to see what happened to them in TRA-03, the final version.

Improved AND deteriorated version (ORI-03→TRA-03)

The translation of ORI-03 is different from the previous stage in that when there already exists a translated version, it is a standard assumption that the text only needs to be retranslated to the extent that the original is changed. In other words, the planning unit calculates the sum total of the text parts that have changed, the translation brief contains this total number and the deadline is set accordingly. This is also the amount of credit the translator can benefit from the task. This procedure thus sends a clear signal to the translators that reworking on the entire text to achieve a polished final version is not encouraged nor rewarded. If those parts of text not indicated for retranslation are also revised, the extra work is not directly appreciated. To account for this in the analysis, the categorization of shifts needs to be somewhat different from the previous versions. The standard, expected state of affairs would be that when there is a change in ORI-03 (with respect to ORI-02), there is also a similar change in TRA-03 (with respect to TRA-02). Departures from this pattern would be unexpected, and thus counted as 'shifts'.

One set of shifts consists of those cases where the original changes but the translation does not. This can happen for various reasons. For example, some of the changes have no bearing on the Finnish because the first translation also covers the semantic field of the changed expression. (In these cases there is also sometimes an 'apparent change', a change for the sake of changing in the translation, although the previous version would have been sufficient.) Interestingly, however, this category also includes cases where the change had already been made in TRA-02. In other words, the translator had been so in tune with the drafting process that he or she had anticipated the changes before the writers produced them. These are fairly small details, often related to readability, but they are an interesting indication of integrated thinking in drafting and translating.

Because the procedure does not support extensive retranslation, the number of changes in the translation not triggered by a change in the original is highly significant. All the work beyond the calculated total number of changes can be seen as voluntary extra effort on the part of the translator (since it does not show in the production figures). A large number of small corrections and improvements belong to this category, counterbalancing the less than optimal congruence in sentence structure that has sometimes been caused by changes triggered by a change in the source text.

Some of the mistranslations found in TRA-02 were corrected in TRA-03, either in the category of extra effort or because there was a new wording in the original. However, most of them stayed. I find slips and errors a normal part of translation work. It depends on the process as to how well they can be eliminated from the final version. Since the drafting and translating process does not include a stage for implementing finishing touches and stylistic revisions before publication, the quality of the end product depends on the previous stages of the process. To eliminate slips and idiosyncratic errors, another pair of eyes is essential. This is why the Finnish unit has emphasized revision. Both focus groups mentioned that they are very proud of their exceptionally strict internal peer revision system in the Finnish unit(s) and adamantly insisted that each document goes through this system before it is released (cf. Wagner et al. 2002: 86). However, as they told me, there is not always time for a comparative reading of the source text and the translation. As I mentioned before, in this case document, the majority of errors were not easily discernible without that sort of comparison. It seems that while the translators are highly motivated to conduct revision, the drafting process offers limited possibilities for a thorough reworking. To ensure the necessary resources for high-quality documents, it might be advisable to add a separate final round of revision in both the drafting and the translating process of out-going documents, at least for the high-priority ones (similar to the final revision stage carried out by jurist-linguists for legislation). Since the English Unit already offers revision services, this pre-publication stage could be entirely accommodated in the DGT.

Translation process: summary

Analysis of the drafting and translating process of this case document reveals an institutional 'group mind' among those involved. The tendencies towards both added readability *and* added institutionalization are visible in all stages. At least in this text, one can discern a 'law of growing institutionalization': each subsequent version takes the features one step further. The more the text is processed, the further it is from being perceived as 'natural' language and the more the role of the Commission gets emphasized. Since the translated text has been processed two times more than the original, the translation appears to be even more institutionalized than the English. This finding seems to corroborate Mason's analysis of his data (texts from the European Parliament). Mason found a general tendency in the translations to move further in the direction of the meanings translators perceived in the original (2003: 184).

In this communication, one apparent direction is towards increased institution-alization, and the translation takes that trait even further than the original.

Although, as we saw in Chapters 4 and 5, the translator is both physically and mentally removed from the drafting process, the force of institutionaliza-tion seems to be the same. The translator is not an agent of change but rather an institutional actor. However, the translator not being familiar with the twists and turns of the earlier versions, the translation sometimes turns to abandoned expressions. The process also allocates less than perfect resources for the revision of both the final original text and the translations, thus reducing the quality of the end product (see also Wagner et al. 2002: 80-81).

The change of language also introduces new shifts in the case document. Resistance towards new coinages in the education policy in the Finnish lan-guage, the simplified structures of the Finnish translation, and the shifting tenor of the directives (see section 6.4 below) present at least potential differences in both the ideational and the interpersonal levels of the English and the Finnish versions of the final document.

6.4 From 'shouldness' to 'maybeness'?

Modality makes possible the monitoring of both the degree of the Commis-sion's commitment to particular processes as well as the degree of its power of mandate towards particular actors. Through modalities, one can thus analyze the power relations and hierarchies between the communicating partners. Many official texts include a directive function: they are written for the purpose of affecting the receivers' behaviour, of telling them how and what they should do. Rick Iedema (1997) has described this feature using the term 'shouldness'. This feature is also typical of many Commission texts. Although the case text has been labelled a "communication", or "tiedonanto" [information+giving], indicating that the Commission is merely disseminating information, in practice it has a strong directive function. The different groups of receivers, however, occupy a different position with respect to the Commission, and it is thus necessary to employ different lexical means to convey 'shouldness' to them.

All actors in the text are put in their hierarchical places. Differences in the Commission mandate are clearly discernible in how they are directed to particular ways of action in the future:

> the Commission will... (when the Commission sets targets to itself)
> Member States should....
> the social partners are invited to...

The case document is on the field of education, which has been left for each member state's own jurisdiction. This is perhaps why member states are also occasionally addressed in a more subtle manner ("Member States are invited to..."), but the most common modal verb for directing member states is "should", which in turn is seldom used for other actors who are not directly subordinate to the Commission, at least not without any hedges ("social partners are invited to . . . and should also..."). Deviations from this system of shouldness tactics tend to get corrected in later versions:

> social partners should (ORI-00) → are invited to agree (ORI-01)
> the Commission should (ORI-02) → will, by the end of 2003 (ORI-03)

The translation of "should" in the Finnish version adds a new angle to the tactics. In the independent reading I had paid attention to the unnatural-looking number of the conditional form in the Finnish text. Comparison between the source text and the translation showed that it had almost without exception been triggered by the modal verb "should" in the original. There is a simple explanation for this systematic rendering of "should" with a conditional form in Finnish: norms. In one of the focus groups, the accepted translation of "should" came up as an example of in-house norms:

C:	It [the differences between EU institutions] also shows in that I had to, was it yesterday or the day before yesterday when I again went to ask A that, that hrrmmm, 'olisi', 'tulisi', 'pitäisi' [three more or less equivalent Finnish conditional forms], one of these three is forbidden here but now again I cannot remember...
B:	(whispering) 'tulisi'
	(laughter)
C:	'tulisi', yeah, and, and well in the parliament it was 'olisi' which was not allowed.

There exists a rather strict system of always rendering "should" as "olisi" or "pitäisi" (in the Commission, that is). Since the system is not easily rationalizable, translators do not always (remember to) follow it. My case document, for example, also includes the 'forbidden' form "tulisi", but I also found a few cases of shifting to the imperative form. More important than the choice between these three options, however, is the outcome of the decision of making a conditional form the suggested equivalent of "should". In all three options, the Finnish conditional form carries with it connotations of non-existent or ineffectual planning (i.e., that something should be done ...). The contemporary meanings of the conditional in Finnish indicate intentionality, predictivity and optative mood ("if only..."; Kauppinen 1998). In short, rather than shouldness, the Finnish conditional may in fact imply 'maybe-ness' (cf. Iedema 1997).

The high frequency of this modal form in the translation creates a confusing feeling of hesitance: Member States should be doing all kinds of things, but whether these will ever actualize remains uncertain.

In English, "should" can be used to convey conditionality (e.g., "Should there be any problems, call me"), and the suggested translation is thus not 'wrong', but in its most frequent use "should" expresses deontic modality (cf. "ought") and is used in indirect directives. This is how I interpret the use of "should" in this communication. Furthermore, expressing directives with a conditional form is not a typical feature of Finnish official texts, although it is sometimes used to soften the tone of necessity or obligation (Hakanen 1993; see also Heikkinen et al. 2000: 140; cf. Matthiessen 2001: 102). The Finnish version can thus be seen to employ a grammatical metaphor (see Halliday 1985: 332): directives are expressed by the conditional form. In other words, the Finnish audience is directed in a softer manner than the English. Does a non-shifting translation equivalent thus result in a shift in tenor from shouldness towards maybe-ness?

6.5 Conclusions: Us and them

An analysis of the drafting and translation process shows that the majority of the shifts that take place have fairly little to do with the actual content of the document but these shifts play a significant role in determining how the text connects with its addressees. In other words, the way in which particular linguistic resources are employed or discarded affects the relationship between the writer and the reader and has further implications concerning the degree of commitment and emphasis on the propositions expressed in the text.

Through the interpersonal shifts that take place during the drafting and translating process of this case document, the writer (i.e., the Commission) emphasizes its own position. This general tendency has been identified in administrative texts. In these texts, the writer often assumes the role of the knowledgeable party that has the power to define and orchestrate things, viewing the reality (the ideational meaning) and the readers (the interpersonal meaning) from above. The institutional writer sets the rules, acts as the referee and assumes the role of the star player (Heikkinen et al. 2000: 204).

It has been argued that the entire participatory approach advocated by the Commission is merely another means of securing its star player role: the new procedures put the Commission in a central position as a policy-broker and help it regain the ground that it has recently lost to the European Parliament (Abels 2002: 13). Bora and Hausendorf (2006: 26, 42) also suggest that we need to analyze what happens to the images of self and others during the procedure. They maintain that catch words such as "citizenship" must find an echo in the communicated images, or else they remain an inanimate formal covering. In the light of this case document, the participatory rhetoric appears rather vacuous. This is because the citizens are ceremoniously glorified, but the star player role is reserved for the Commission who views the citizens, the educational system and the readers from above and whose view of reality is not to be questioned. The counterpart of this omniscient institutional writer in the text is an implied institutional reader who understands and accepts this view, and who speaks the same institutional language (Heikkinen et al. 2000: 206).

The institutional writer and the institutional reader together form a unanimous group: us. The institutional translator, I would argue, is more 'us' than the translators' own discourse (see chapter 5) would lead one to believe: they are not explicitly included in the in-group, neither in the framework documents, nor in the translation process, but their strategies tend towards institutionally accepted decisions. The citizens (the implied 'them' in the text) are also given an institutional role in the text: they are or they should all be (potential) learners. On the surface level of the text, 'learners' are emphatically active ("promoting real active citizenship!"), but a closer reading reveals that they are the object of activity, not addressed readers of the communication. They are definitely not 'us'. Although the text is apparently also directed at interested citizens, both the officialese and the educational policy jargon accommodate the text to a particular institutional culture, alienating those who are not members of that in-group. A similar alienation effect was reported by a group of Italian history teachers who read the Italian version of a white paper on education: all the teachers admitted that they had had serious problems in understanding even the most basic information because of the complicated sentence structure and unusual lexical choices. The teachers complained that the text was only understandable to those readers who were knowledgeable about the topic and familiar with the convoluted rhetoric (Tosi 2003: 58). In other words, members of the very professional group targeted by the white paper found themselves excluded from the in-group of 'us'.

It is temptingly easy to criticize this institutionalized discourse, but, as Rick Iedema (1997: 95-96) warns us, we may forget that its subtlety and complexity are there to serve two functions: the organization of human activity (shouldness) and institutional positioning (interpersonal distance). Demands for increased user-friendliness or linguistic simplicity may result in 'cosmetic democratization' (remember the greeting 'Hei Kaisa!'): in institutional settings where power relations are, and will remain, unequal, the covert markers may become all the more potent as the overt markers of power asymmetry become less evident (Fairclough 1992: 203). As we saw in the analysis above, adding readability and accessibility is by no means a straightforward task.

7. Net Results

7.1 Rules, norms and beliefs: the question of culture in institutional translation

My main objective in the preceding chapters has been to weave a tight net of life and work at the Finnish translation unit of the European Commission in Luxembourg. This case study of one translation unit was also designed to shed light on institutional translation in general. While each individual case is always unique, some findings may be applicable to other situations of institutional *in-house* translation (freelance translation is a different story altogether), or they can at least function as testable hypotheses for future research. Returning to the three pillars of institutions introduced in Chapter 2, we can draw some conclusions from the regulative, normative and cultural cognitive perspectives.

Within the regulative framework of EU translation, the staff regulations are a central instrument. These regulations in no way distinguish translators from the other A-level officials: their rights, duties and remunerations are equal. Their institutional career is highly regulated from recruitment to retirement. In contrast, practical, everyday work appears to be rather unregulated, and there are few guidelines as to preferred translation strategies. The normative pillar, then, consists of norms and values. Values are the conceptions of what is preferred and desirable; norms are guidelines for achieving these ends. The data from all three levels indicates a shared value: readability. Policy papers, translators and drafters all appear to be striving towards this end. Both the regulative and the normative perspective indicate that translation is an integrated system: translators are not singled out in institutional regulations, and the central values are shared across the different professional groups.

The cultural cognitive approach indicates a more complicated picture. As a professional group, translators may have a tendency to view themselves as detached from other officials, creating an internally coherent society with few external ties within the institution. This tendency is enforced by a similar tendency on the policy level of ignoring the resources of translators and relegating them to an instrumental and invisible role. In comparison with the integrating aspects of the regulative and normative pillars, the mental construction of translators and translation both by the translators themselves and by others emphasize difference and detachment. Similar barriers to socialization and lack of visibility may well apply to translators in many other institutional settings as well. The professional role of translators as mediators, with its ethics of impartiality, may leave the translators susceptible to a certain alienation even within in-house settings where their official status effectively excludes impartiality.

In Chapter 3 above, I quoted questions posed by Anthony Pym (2000: 16) on the EU translators' institutional role and professional identity: Do they work in the name of their languages and cultures, or is there an EU interculture?; When the crunch comes, which way do they decide?; Is their professional vision inward toward the intercultural institutions, or outward toward receivers who are not in intercultural positions? These questions can now be at least tentatively answered. On the basis of this case, it seems that the translators are not entirely socialized into the Commission, but have rather developed their own cultural niche(s) within it. They are not, however, intercultural agents in Pym's sense of the term, since they are not detached from the institution for which they work. They do not work to serve the national interests of their home country but to serve the institution, although they do not feel they quite belong to it. Their professional vision is therefore divided: they wish to reach out to their readers, but feel they cannot quite accomplish that. When the crunch comes, I would argue, they are likely to stay on the side of the institution – not out of love, perhaps, but out of duty.

7.2 Readability

One of the most striking features of the translation practice of the European Commission is the issue of readability. As we saw in the preceding chapters, there exists a unanimous and explicit normative call for readability across the data. The Commission documents call for understandable drafting and information adapted to local needs; the translators argue that translators always take their readers into consideration and agonize if they feel they cannot do that; the draft versions – both originals and translations – contain ample evidence of attempts to improve the readability of the document. In translation studies, norms have been a centre of attention in institutionally oriented approaches (see Chapter 2). According to Gideon Toury's (1995) well-known definition, translation is a norm-governed activity. Norms, then, are the translation of the general values shared by a community into performance instructions. Norms also bridge the micro world of individual actors and the larger institutional framework (Nee 1998: 3). The shared norm of readability, it would seem, guides and directs the translators' routine decisions towards translation solutions that are considered reader-friendly.

Socialized norms result in observable regularities of behaviour (Toury 1995: 55). The products and outcomes of these norm-governed instances of behaviour can be studied, although the norms themselves are not directly observable. With regard to translational norms, the translations themselves are the primary source of information. For example, underlying norms can be inferred through an analysis of shifts. According to Toury, extratextual pronouncements are secondary by products, and their trustworthiness is limited (ibid.: 65). However, Toury (ibid.: 58) also differentiates between preliminary norms and operational norms. Whereas preliminary norms concern the existence and nature of translation policy, operational norms direct the decisions made during the actual translation process. It would seem logical to assume that operational norms can be observed from the products of behaviour, in this case the draft versions and translations, and preliminary norms from the more general framework discussions, in this case, the European Commission policy documents and the translators' discourse. It would also seem logical to assume that preliminary norms somehow govern and constrain the nature of operational norms: if there is a preliminary preference towards readability, one could then assume and expect operational norms to strive towards this aim. Evidence from all three subsets of data above, however, suggests that parallel to the explicit and shared norm of readability, there also exists another tendency identifiable from the textual products. I have labelled this tendency 'institutionalization', and argued that it affects interpersonal relations between the Commission and the readers.

According to the bipartite differentiation put forward by Victor Nee and Paul Ingram, *informal* norms are implicit and monitored via informal mechanisms, while *formal* norms are explicit rules relying on formal enforcement mechanisms (1998: 19). Nee and Ingram argue that in organizations not operating on competitive markets (e.g., government agencies), formal organizational rules are largely ceremonial, and that informal norms, independent of this ceremonial structure, will tend to guide the day-to-day business (1998: 35). In the context of EU translation, this would imply a rift between the abstract, preliminary norms at the DGT/Commission level and the nitty-gritty of the operational level in the translation units. Following Nee and Ingram's categorization, this tendency of institutionalization could be defined as an informal norm. In this case, the informal norm conflicts with the more formal norm, effectively blocking the desired outcome the formal norm aims to foster. Incongruence between formal and informal norms makes them more costly to monitor and enforce (Nee 1998: 9). This can be easily verified by looking at the resources and manpower the Commission has lately invested in its attempts to improve readability.

A normative approach can be of some use in explaining the data. However, a more accurate explanation can be found if we accept that in addition to being governed by norms, translation is also guided by other factors. In sociology, the central role of norms in human behaviour has recently been questioned, and the use of the concept outside sociology has been labelled as mere "sociological spicing" (Gronow 2006). At the same time, the role of habits and (reasoned) routines has been emphasized. It might be fruitful to perceive institutionalization as an accidental outcome of numerous routine or habitual decisions. One could in fact argue that the explicit norm of readability in my various sets of data exists *because of* the tendency of institutionalization. In other words, the norm only comes into being to solve a problematic situation. Norms may be a central feature of human societies, but in our daily life we do not only respond to value judgements. Most of the time, we may actually deal with our daily chores rather routinely and unreflectively. "Rather than calculating the future consequences of alternative sets of action", Nee argues, "actors rely on rules of thumb and established routines" (1998: 10). Similarly, the Finnish sociologist Pertti Alasuutari (2004: 50 and passim.) maintains that *tacit routines* – not norms – are the backbone of social order. He argues that the need to evoke and enforce norms in social situations is a sign of crisis. As for EU translation, it seems that numerous tacit routines and pragmatic material solutions could rather accidentally contribute to an outcome no one desires: less than optimal translated communication.

In the course of my analysis, the pervasiveness of reader-orientedness across my data took me by surprise. I was prepared to find a more schematic picture: I quite expected that the translators would argue for readability, but I did not anticipate finding so many practical applications of it in the transla-tions, and even less so in the draft originals. I also envisioned the translators as being completely invisible in the policy documents (and so they were, but there were numerous openings for the DGT to seize) and did not foresee the emphasis on readers and communication to be so high on the policy agenda. By triangulating the results of three subsets of data, I thought, I could reveal the rifts and tensions *between* them. Instead, my triangulation exercise seems to have revealed three subsets equally torn by *internal* tensions. The problem of creating an affinity with the readers in spite of the institutional distance runs through all the three levels of analysis. The institutional context imposes itself, and even though the outspoken norm is towards readability, the institutional routines and processes enhance institutionalization.

The interplay of institutionality and readability across the different subsets of data raises interesting questions concerning triangulation. In traditional scientific thinking, triangulation is seen as cross-validation, as a way of con-firming the findings of one method by validating them with the help of another method or new set of data. The idea is that triangulation can help you make a stronger case. This view is perhaps too optimistic: additional methods and new kinds of data may help solve some problems but they also often open up new unexplored avenues for research that the first method did not illuminate, or additional analysis may even contradict the evidence acquired before. Combined methods can thus also add to the confusion and lead to a *less* solid perception of the problem under study (see Fern 2001: 176).

How you see triangulation, and to what extent you are worried about a potential lack of convergence, reflects your world view in a manner similar to the different research perspectives on organizational culture as classified by

Joanne Martin (2002; see Ch. 3). If your approach to scientific information is integrationist, you may tend to expect triangulation to solidify the results, and any residual incongruence is then a cause for worry. A proponent of the differential perspective, on the other hand, might find it fruitful to contrast the different kinds of data to evaluate the different methods and researcher interventions and power differentials behind the results. In contrast to the integrative approach, in fragmentationalist research triangulation might be used specifically to *expose* the contradictions and paradoxes that, according to a fragmentationalist world view, are inherent in any slice of reality we set out to investigate. In such cases, the role of triangulation and multiple methods is in fact the opposite of the way it has been traditionally understood. Incongruent results are then expected, or even desired and teased out, and the discrepancies are used to develop new insights that might not have been accessible with any single method (Martin J. 2002: 235). In this case, the question of triangulation is confused: on the one hand (and contrary to my rather fragmentationalist presumptions) the different sets of data and different methods tell the same story; on the other hand, the story they all repeat is a story of incongruence, of a continuous battle between loyalties to the readers and to the institution.

The benefit of mixing different kinds of data and viewpoints lies in understanding their tensions and interrelatedness. The translators' own views of their roles are seasoned by a look at the official documents which *both* ignore them completely *and* offer them a potentially significant role. Similarly, translators' laments of not being able to take the readers into account are balanced by an analysis of the case translation where the translator obviously does a lot precisely to enhance readability. Furthermore, looking at both the drafting and translating processes reveals not only the peculiarities of translation but also the similarities between monolingual drafting and translating. In short, a comprehensive approach helps in situating the individual pieces of information into a larger picture and in avoiding easy simplifications.

7.3 Recognition

Outsiders often – quite rationally – assume that the in-house translators of the European Commission work in an international and multicultural environment and in liaison with other Commission officials. Some readers may thus have been somewhat surprised by the degree of isolation and monolingual compartmentalization that the translators experienced. Translators are geographically separated from other officials; their offices are located either in Luxembourg or in the outskirts of Brussels, and the organization structure divides them according to language instead of, say, forming teams of all translators working for a particular DG. In the everyday life of the Commission, other officials do not regularly meet and mingle with translators, and translation remains an invisible practice to them. Translators, consequently, do not feel that they are an integral part of the organization, but rather feel like a "necessary evil". This invisibility is also reflected in the Commission documents focusing on communication and reaching out to European citizens: no attention is paid to the translation processes involved.

(In)visibity has been high on the agenda of translation studies from the 1990s onwards. In his two provocative monographs (1995, 1998), Lawrence Venuti stated that the translators' textual invisibility (fluent and transparent style) and their "shadowy existence" in Anglo-American culture (Venuti 1995: 8) both contribute to translators' unfavourable treatment in copyright law and their lack of recognition in criticisms and remunerations alike. Venuti's argument links invisibility with both cultural and economic misrecognition, and he promotes a new, emancipatory and resistant culture of translation. This project of visibility has been very influential, also and particularly outside its original Anglo-American sphere (see Koskinen 2000b).

Nancy Fraser's critique of the politics of recognition adds interesting viewpoints to the discussions of visibility. "Identity models", she argues, are often flawed since they result in reification, producing a simplified group identity which denies the multiplicity of the identifications and the cross-pulls of people's various affiliations (Fraser 2000: 112). Focusing on group identity prevents us from perceiving in-group differences and individual agendas. My small sample of EU translators indicates that educational background,[1] for example, can rather dramatically influence their views and values.

Nancy Fraser proposes an alternative approach that focuses on the question of social status ("status model") and recognition. Instead of group-specific identity, Fraser emphasizes the status of the individual group members as full partners in social interaction. Misrecognition, then, is to be understood in the sense of being prevented from participating as a peer in social life. Misrecognition can be juridified in formal law, or it can be institutionalized through policies, administrative codes or professional practice. The status model thus focuses on the institutionalized patterns of cultural value, assessing whether they constitute various actors as peers.

> When, in contrast, they constitute some actors as inferior, excluded, wholly other, or simply invisible – in other words, as less than full partners in social interaction – then we can speak of misrecognition and status subordination. (Fraser 2000: 113)

Commission policy statements, which make no reference to translators, and professional practices in which the translators are detached from both their

---

[1] A traditional variant among professional translators: there are many routes to this profession.

in-house clients and outside readers seem to provide evidence of inferiority, invisibility and otherness. However, the case of EU translators adds new complexity to the often assumed causal link between cultural misrecognition and unequal economic distribution. EU translators may be culturally mis-recognized in their professional community, but in economic and juridical terms, they are accepted as peers. Their salary levels, terms of employment, social benefits, as well as their duties and restrictions, are exactly the same as those of others. Discussing the complex relationship between recognition and distribution, Fraser concludes that "not all economic injustice can be over-come by recognition alone" (2000: 119). On the basis of this case it should be added that the opposite also applies: not all problems of cultural misrecogni-tion can be overcome by equal distribution of financial benefits alone. This raises serious questions on the pervasiveness of the invisible and subordinate model of translation historically, geographically and across different fields of translation. Economically, EU translators are top professionals. Neverthe-less, in their everyday work they seem to suffer from the age-old translators' problems arising from misrecognition.

7.4 Towards reflexive practice

The status model seeks "institutional remedies for institutionalized harms" (Fraser 2000). For EU translators, this would entail reinforced input in com-munication work and new professional practices to increase their contact with clients. The policy documents that stress the need to communicate the European message do not emphasize the pivotal role of the translators. This lack of awareness may, however, also reflect the instrumental role assumed by the DGT itself rather than just the ignorance of policy makers. In fact, lack of proactive involvement has been a predominant feature of high-level DGT discourses: there seems to be a lack of vision as to the future role of translators. The DGT has been slow in responding to the implicit call for a more active engagement put forward in recent communication strategies, and the mission statements analyzed in Chapter 4 offer little strategic guidance for transla-tors. A more active approach would give support to translators in combating institutionalization and could serve as a tool for improving communication. As long as the Commission relies primarily on translated communication (as it will continue to do in the foreseeable future), the quality of the translations will be crucial for its success. Moreover, unless the Commission succeeds in reaching and convincing the intended audiences of its normal (translated) communication flow, the new communications people and goodwill ambas-sadors it plans to employ in its field offices will probably remain a cosmetic resource of limited value.

Since the translators are physically and mentally removed from the rest of the drafting process, they perhaps take their passive and instrumental role too much for granted. The revolution of the DGT could also begin from the grassroots level if the translators decided to fully exploit their capacities. They are, after all, A-level officials, members of the group that can and should be expected to take a leading role with regard to the development of the EU institutions. This potential for initiative could be tapped by the translators.

> The Translation Service should become more responsible. It is the Directorate General with the highest percentage of officials with a university degree. Translators are very competent in language matters, but they are too shy and too passive in general. [. . .] they do not see themselves as potential managers, as people who should think and take full responsibility for the texts they produce in view of the decision-making process of the Commission. In many DGs, even C-grade secretaries have more responsibilities than translators do. I think it is very important for the future of the Translation Service that translators become active partners. (Ex-translator Monique Scottini, in Wagner et al 2000: 125)

In the above quotation, Scottini refers to the future of the DGT. I take it that she implies the threat of outsourcing all translation to private firms unless the DGT can demonstrate the added value of in-house translation. This is a realistic fear: the outsourcing of in-house translation has been a current trend in the commercial markets for quite some time, and public organizations seem to be following suit. Recently there have been news reports of, for example, the UN planning to outsource its translation and documentation jobs and of the national Finnish Broadcasting Company planning to transfer the dubbing of animated films to private companies. Privatization of this type is often bad news for translators: the in-house translators of the European Union institutions have permanent well-paid jobs and good retirement benefits; freelancers for the EU are subject to competitive bidding, and often end up working as subcontractors.

Recent news from the DGT indicate that the translation service has indeed taken up new initiatives: it has set up a new 'web translation' unit to enhance communication with EU citizens, and increased the number of staff translators in its field offices (with the task of 'localizing' the messages to local audiences). The new multilingualism portfolio in the Commission[2] effective since the beginning of 2007 creates new expectations of bringing added visibility and political weight to the foundational translating and interpreting activities of the EU institutions. It was not possible to include an analysis of

---

[2] See http://ec.europa.eu/commission_barroso/orban/index_en.htm.

these promising new developments in this study. A contemporary activity is a moving target: it does not stand still while the researcher is busy at work analyzing the previous set of data. While this is frustrating for the researcher, it is good news for the institution. To quote the present Director General of the DGT: "At the end of the day, it is also significant to realise that it is possible to move this ship despite its size and complexity, and adapt it to changing realities" (Lönnroth 2007).

Recognition and appreciation are valuable goals in themselves, but an even more fundamental reason for more active involvement of the translators in the processes can be seen to come from the sphere of professional ethics. No matter how much they wish to remain detached from the institution they are serving, translators *are* an integral part of its political processes. The responsibility *is* there. The inherent ambivalence between readability and institutionalization in the translators' work makes it more necessary for them to take an active role. When negotiating between the two opposing poles, there are no clear-cut rules to follow; the fundamental undecidability between them calls for increased reflexivity (Koskinen 2000b: 26-30; 114).

It is, however, equally important to keep in mind the need for reflexivity in research. One major benefit of ethnographic approaches is that they force the researcher to constantly reflect and reassess her own role and place in the project. Many translation scholars have some experience of practical translation work, and it is not uncommon to use this experience in research. Combining the two is not, however, straightforward. Personal experience is an asset in research, but it also poses risks and difficulties. These risks can involve split loyalties towards colleagues in the work place on the one hand and academic objectivity on the other. In addition, a conflict of roles may arise. Moreover, the tacit knowledge acquired by firsthand experience is often difficult to integrate in research reports.

From the very beginning of my project, I found my own position – that of an earlier insider turned into an outsider – somewhat troublesome. I needed to locate myself within the project, and I had to find a way of dealing with my own personal experiences. Equally important, I needed to find ways to make sure the participants did not feel exploited in the process. And thirdly, I needed to come to terms with my role in relation to the European Commission: in what ways is it my business – or the business of those funding my research – to offer the Commission any advice as to how they could improve their ability to get their messages across?

Ethnography is not an easy choice for a researcher: it is slow and time-consuming, and it requires a high level of personal involvement; the inherent aim of completeness leaves the researcher with a sense of unavoidable failure, and the typical reporting format of a monograph does not enhance their academic career at a time when all that really counts seems to be the number of international refereed articles in one's list of publications. But there is also a bonus side. The richness of everyday reality is a fascinating object of study, offering endless surprises and new challenges throughout the project and beyond. Research situated on the grass-root level of the reality of the contemporary field of professional translation is also motivating, and addressing issues arising from real life can enhance the researcher's feelings of meaningfulness.

I hope I have succeeded in conveying something of the complexity of the reality the EU translators face in their daily work. It is, however, obvious that there are holes in every net. In weaving this net, I have left a multitude of aspects aside. It remains the task of future research to find out what life is like in other translation units, and to compare it with other kinds of institutional translation. There would also be scope for a major corpus study of EU translation across languages and institutions. Among the numerous possible topics of future research, I particularly wish to point one out: the role of human-computer interaction in (EU) translation. Not only is the EU translators' work thoroughly computerized, but so are their contacts: the requesters and the Finnish authorities are contacted via e-mail, as are their friends and family in Finland. The Finnish newspapers are online, and so is the Finnish-Luxembourg Society. This, of course, could be said of the daily reality of many of us, but it is surely worth asking how the computerization and digitalization of our relations affects our (cultural) affiliations. After all, the nets we are caught in are increasingly virtual.

Appendix 1

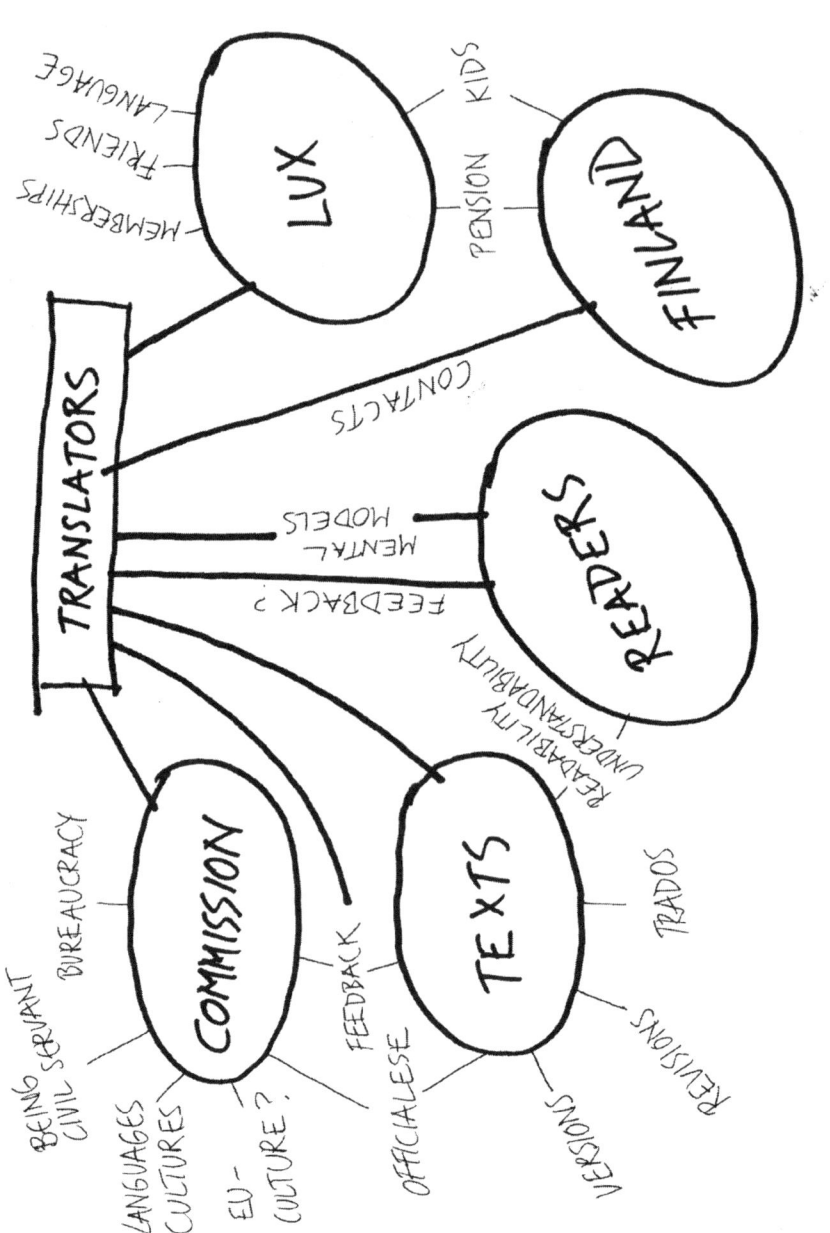

Appendix 2

QUESTIONNAIRE

Circle the most accurate choice or fill in the answers to open questions.

1 Background

female   male

age group   20-29   30-39   40-49   50-59   60-

Education   1   translator training
             2   other language education
             3   other

Work experience as a translator before the Commission _____ years

Translator in the European Commission   _____ years

My home is in
1   Luxembourg
2   Finland
3   France
4   Germany
5   Belgium
6   elsewhere (specify):_____

In Luxembourg I live in
1   private house/apartment
2   rented house/apartment
3   hotel etc.
4   not at all

I feel I am primarily
1   Finnish
2   European
3   Luxembourgish
4   other (specify): _____

In my daily interactions I use the following languages:_____

_____
_____
_____

If you do not have family, you can move on to section 3.

2 Family

If you are married or living together with someone, is your spouse
1   Finnish
2   Finnish, met in the EU context
3   Non-Finnish EU official
4   Luxembourgish
5   other

If you have children, are they (circle multiple choises if applicable)
1   at home with the other parent
2   at home, with an au pair (nationality of the au pair: _____)
3   in family day care outside home (nationality of the care-taker:_____)
3   in the EU nursery
4   in a local nursery
5   in Europe shcool
6   in a local school
7   elsewhere (specify: _____)

The nationality of the best friend of my child is

     1. child _____
     2. child _____
     3. child _____

In my opinion the identity of my child/children is _____

_____
_____
_____
_____

in their daily interaction they use the following languages:

_____
_____
_____

3 Work

Describe the Commission with a few words

_____

_____

Describe your work with a few words

_____

_____

Describe Luxembourg with a few words

_____

_____

In my work I am in contact with

Finnish translator colleagues	daily	weekly	sometimes	never
Other translator colleagues	daily	weekly	sometimes	never
Requesters	daily	weekly	sometimes	never
Source text writers	daily	weekly	sometimes	never
Finnish EU officials	daily	weekly	sometimes	never
Other EU officials	daily	weekly	sometimes	never
Experts in Finland	daily	weekly	sometimes	never
Finnish language professionals	daily	weekly	sometimes	never
Users of translations in Commission	daily	weekly	sometimes	never
Users of translations in Finland	daily	weekly	sometimes	never

My translations are revised by another translator

always	nearly always	fairly often	seldom	never

Why?_____

_____

_____

I get feedback from

Finnish translator colleagues	daily	weekly	sometimes	never
Other translator colleagues	daily	weekly	sometimes	never
Requesters	daily	weekly	sometimes	never
Source text writers	daily	weekly	sometimes	never

Finnish EU officials	daily	weekly	sometimes	never
Other EU officials	daily	weekly	sometimes	never
Experts in Finland	daily	weekly	sometimes	never
Finnish language professionals	daily	weekly	sometimes	never
Users of translations in Commission	daily	weekly	sometimes	never
Users of translations in Finland	daily	weekly	sometimes	never

The amount of feedback is

too little   appropriate   too much

Why?_____

_____

_____

_____

Translation memory tools

1   have made my work easier
2   have made my work harder
3   have not affected my work (neither made it easier nor harder)

Why?_____

_____

_____

_____

In my work I get motivation from/ I find fulfilling

_____

_____

_____

_____

_____

My work is adversely affected/ my motivation is lessened by

_____

_____

_____

_____

_____

Organize the following claims in the order of importance (1=most important, etc.). If you wish, you can add new items.

When translating I mainly aim at

____   keeping the schedule
____   using correct language
____   producing a fluent and readable text
____   making sure that the content is equivalent with the source text
____   following established formulas
____   adapting the text for the Finnish readers
____   renewing the textual practices used in the Commission

____   _____

____   _____

In my opinion the DGT should **primarily** serve

1   the Commission officials
2   the Member States
3   European citizens
4   the ideals of the European union
5   other (specify):_____

4 Relations

Last week I had lunch at work with

Nobody	0	1	2	3	4	5	times
Finnish translator	0	1	2	3	4	5	times
Non-Finnish translator	0	1	2	3	4	5	times
Finnish official	0	1	2	3	4	5	times
Non-Finnish official	0	1	2	3	4	5	times
Other	0	1	2	3	4	5	times

I visit Finland

0   1   2   3   4   5   6   7   8   9   10+   times per year.

In time, visits to Finland have become
less frequent   stayed the same   more frequent

While in Luxembourg I follow the following media:

Finnish newspapers	daily	weekly	sometimes	never
Finnish magazines	daily	weekly	sometimes	never
Finnish radio/tv-programmes	daily	weekly	sometimes	never
Local newspapers (lux)	daily	weekly	sometimes	never
Local magazines (lux)	daily	weekly	sometimes	never
Local radio/tv-programmes (lux)	daily	weekly	sometimes	never
International/foreign newspapers	daily	weekly	sometimes	never
International/foreign magazines	daily	weekly	sometimes	never
International/foreign radio/tv-pr.	daily	weekly	sometimes	never

If there have been changes in your media habits during the years you have stayed in Luxembourg, mark those mediums with (+) which you now follow more than before and those with (–) which you now follow less than before.

During May and June 2004, I have had at my home visitors

1   Finnish relatives/friends
2   Finnish translators or their family members
3   Finnish EU officials or their family members
4   other EU officials or their family members
5   local relatives/friends (from Luxembourg or your country of residence)
6   relatives/friends from elsewhere that from Finland or Luxembourg/ country of residence
7   there have been no visitors

The floor is yours. Describe with your own words how you feel about Finland/ Finns, the Commission and your work there and Luxembourg/the Luxembourgers. You can continue on the other side of this paper. You can also give feedback from this group discussion and questionnaire.

References

Abdallah, Kristiina (forthcoming) *Translation Quality in Production Networks: From Conflict to Cooperation*. Dissertation. University of Tampere.

Abélès, Marc (2000) 'Virtual Europe', in Irène Bellier and Thomas M. Wilson (eds) *An Anthropology of the European Union. Building, Imagining and Experiencing the New Europe*, Oxford and New York: Berg, 31-52.

------, Irène Bellier and Maryon McDonald (1993) 'Approche Anthropologique de la Commission Européenne'. Unpublished report, European Commission.

Abels, Gabriele (2002) 'Experts, Citizens, and Eurocrats – Towards a Policy Shift in the Governance of Biopolitics in the EU', *European Integration online Papers* (EIoP) 6(19), http://eiop.or.at/eiop/texte/2002-019.htp. Accessed 27 June 2006.

Agar, Michael and James MacDonald (1995) 'Focus Groups and Ethnography', *Human Organization* 54(1): 78-86.

Alasuutari, Pertti (2004) *Social Theory and Human Reality*, London: Sage.

------ (2006) 'Merkitys, toiminta ja rakenne sosiologiassa: kulttuurinen näkökulma' (Meaning, action and structure in sociology: a cultural viewpoint), *Sosiologia* 43(2): 79-92.

Arrojo, Rosemary (1995) 'Femisnist, 'Orgasmic' Theories of Translation and Their Contradictions', *TradTerm* 2: 67-75.

Atkinson, Paul (1990) *The Ethnographic Imagination. Textual constructions of reality,* London and New York: Routledge.

------ and Martyn Hammersley (1994) 'Ethnography and Participant Observation', in Norman K. Denzin and Yvonna S. Lincoln (eds) *Handbook of Qualitative Research*, Thousand Oaks: Sage, 248-261.

------ and Amanda Coffey (2003) 'Revisiting the relationship between participant observation and interviewing', in Jaber F. Gubrium and James A. Holstein (eds) *Postmodern Interviewing*, Thousand Oaks: Sage, 109-122.

Bahadir, Şebnem (2004) 'Moving In-Between: The Interpreter as Ethnographer and the Interpreting-Researcher as Anthropologist', *Meta* XLIX (4): 805-821.

Bakhtin, Mikhail (1965/2002) *François Rabelais – keskiajan ja renessanssin nauru,* [Laughter during the Middle Age and Renaissance], trans. Tapani Laine and Paula Nieminen, Helsinki: Like.

Barley, Stephen R. (1991) 'Semiotics and the Study of Occupational and Organizational Culture', in Peter J. Frost, Larry F. Moore, Meryl Reis Luis, Craig C. Lundberg and Joanne Martin (eds) *Reframing Organizational Culture*, Newbury Park: Sage, 39-54.

Behar, Ruth (1996) *The Vulnerable Observer. Anthropology That Breaks Your Heart,* Boston: Beacon Press.

Bellier, Irène (2000) 'The European Union, Identity Politics and the Logic of Interests' Representation', in Irène Bellier and Thomas M. Wilson (eds) *An Anthropology of the European Union. Building, Imagining and Experiencing the New Europe*, Oxford and New York: Berg, 53-73.

------ and Thomas M. Wilson (2000) 'Building, Imagining and Experiencing Europe: Institutions and Identities in the European Union', in Irène Bellier and Thomas M. Wilson (eds) *An Anthropology of the European Union. Building, Imagining and Experiencing the New Europe*. Oxford and New York: Berg, 1-27.

Bhatia, Vijay K. (1999) 'Integrating products, processes, purposes and participants in professional writing', in Christopher N. Candlin and Ken Hyland (eds) *Writing: Texts, Processes and Practices*, London and New York: Longman, 21-39.

Blum-Kulka, Shoshana (1986/2000), 'Shifts of cohesion and coherence in translation', in Lawrence Venuti (ed.) *The Translation Studies Reader*, London and New York: Routledge, 298-313.

Bora, Alfons and Heiko Hausendorf (2006) 'Communicating citizenship and social positioning. Theoretical concepts', in Heiko Hausendorf and Alfons Bora (eds) *Analysing Citizenship Talk. Social positioning in political and legal decision-making processes*, Amsterdam and Philadelphia: John Benjamins, 23-49.

Boyle, Joyceen S. (1994) 'Styles of Ethnography', in Janice M. Morse (ed.) *Critical Issues in Qualitative Research Methods*, Thousand Oaks: Sage, 160-185.

Buzelin, Hélène (2005) 'Opening the Black Box: Towards a Study of Translation as a Production Process', paper presented at the conference 'Translating and Interpreting as a Social Practice', University of Graz, 5-7 May 2005.

Calzada Pérez, María (2001) 'A three-level methodology for descriptive-explanatory Translation Studies', *Target* 13(2): 203-239.

Campbell, Marie (2003) 'Dorothy Smith and knowing the world we live in', *Journal of Sociology and Social Welfare*, March: 1-13.

Candlin, Christopher N. and Ken Hyland (eds) (1999) *Writing: Texts, Processes and Practices*, London and New York: Longman.

Carey, Martha Ann (1994) 'The Group Effect in Focus Groups: Planning, Implementing, and Interpreting Focus Group Research', in Janice M. Morse (ed.) *Critical Issues in Qualitative Research Methods*, Thousand Oaks: Sage, 225-241.

Catford, J.C. (1965) *A Linguistic Theory of Translation: An Essay in Applied Linguistics*, Oxford: Oxford University Press.

Catteral, M. and P. Maclaran (1997) 'Focus Group Data and Qualitative Analysis Programs: Coding the Moving Picture as Well as the Snapshots', *Sociological Research Online* 2(1), http://www.soucresonline.org.uk/2/1/6.html, Accessed 31 March 2005.

Chamberlain, Lori (1998) 'Gender metaphorics in translation', in Mona Baker (ed.) *Routledge Encyclopedia of Translation Studies*, London and New York: Routledge, 93-96.

Chesterman, Andrew (1997) *Memes of Translation. The Spread of Ideas in Translation Theory*, Amsterdam and Philadelphia: John Benjamins.

------ (1998) *Contrastive Functional Analysis,* Amsterdam and Philadelphia: John Benjamins.

Christophory, Jul (1998) 'Lëtzebuergesch and the Overall Language Situation in Luxembourg', *T&T* 3: 116-134.

Coffey, Amanda (1999) *The Ethnographic Self. Fieldwork and the Representation of Identity,* Newbury Park: Sage.

Cronin, Michael (2003) *Translation and Globalization*, London and New York: Routledge.

Czarniawska-Joerges, Barbara (1992) *Exploring Complex Organizations. A Cultural Perspective,* Newbury Park: Sage.

Czarniawska, Barbara (1997) *Narrating the Organization. Dramas of Institutional Identity*, Chicago: University of Chicago Press.

Diamond, Jared (2003) *Tykit, taudit ja teräs. Ihmisen yhteiskuntien kohtalot* [Orig. Guns, Germs, and Steel. The Fates of Human Societies] trans. Kimmo Pietiläinen, Helsinki: Terra Cognita.

Diriker, Ebru (2004*) De-/Re-contextualizing Conference Interpreting: Interpreters in the Ivory Tower?* Amsterdam and Philadelphia: John Benjamins.

Dollerup, Cay (2001) 'The language scene in South Africa', *Language International* 13(1): 34-36.

Drew, Paul and John Heritage (1992/1998) 'Analyzing Talk at Work', in Paul Drew and John Heritage (eds) *Talk at Work. Interaction in institutional settings,* Cambridge: Cambridge University Press, 3-65.

Eipper, Chris (1998) 'Anthropology and cultural studies: difference, ethnography and theory', *The Australian Journal of Anthropology* 9(3): 310-326.

Eskola, Sari (2002) *Syntetisoivat rakenteet käännössuomessa. Suomennetun kaunokirjallisuuden ominaispiirteiden tarkastelua korpusmenetelmillä.* [Synthetising Structures in Translated Finnish. A Corpus-based Analysis of the Special Features of Finnish Literary Translations], Publications of the Humanities 30, Joensuu: University of Joensuu.

Fairclough, Norman (1992) *Discourse and Social Change,* Cambridge: Polity Press.

------ (1995) *Critical Discourse Analysis. The Critical Study of Language,* Harlow: Longman.

Feldman, Martha S. (1991) 'The Meanings of Ambiguity: Learning from Stories and Metaphors', in Peter J. Frost, Larry F. Moore, Meryl Reis Luis, Craig C. Lundberg and Joanne Martin (eds) *Reframing Organizational Culture*, Newbury Park: Sage, 145-156.

Fern, Edward F. (2001) *Advanced Focus Group Research*, Newbury Park: Sage.

Fiol, C. Marlene, Mary Jo Hatch and Karen Golden-Biddle (1998) 'Organizational Culture and Identity: What's the Difference Anyway?', in David A. Whetten and Paul V. Godfrey (eds) *Organizational Identity. Building Theory Through Conversations* Thousand Oaks: Sage, 56-59.

Flotow, Luise von (1991) 'Feminist Translation: Contexts, Practices and Theories', *TTR* 4(2): 69-84.

Fox, Richard G. and Barbara J. King (eds) (2002) *Anthropology Beyond Culture,* Oxford and New York: Berg.

Fraser, Bill (1997) 'The New Rhetoric. How discourse analysis can help translators', *T&T* 3: 149-179.

Fraser, Nancy (2000) 'Rethinking recognition', *New Left Review* 3: 107-120.

Gile, Daniel (1998) 'Observational Studies and Experimental Studies in the Investigation of Conference Interpreting', *Target* 10(1): 69-93.

------ and Gyde Hansen (2004) 'The editorial process through the looking glass', in Gyde Hansen, Kirsten Malmkjær and Daniel Gile (eds) *Claims, Changes and Challenges in Translation Studies*, Selected Contributions from the EST Congress, Copenhagen 2001, Amsterdam: John Benjamins, 297-306.

Glenn, Philip (2003) *Laughter in Interaction*, Studies in international sociolinguistics 18, Cambridge: Cambridge University Press.

Gronow, Antti (2006) 'Instituutiot taloustieteessä ja sosiologiassa: pragmatistinen kritiikki' (Institutions in economics and sociology: a pragmatistic critique) *Sosiologia* 43(2): 93-106.

Gubrium, Jaber F. and James A. Holstein (2001) 'Introduction. Trying Times, Troubled Selves', in Jaber F. Gubrium and James A. Holstein (eds) *Institutional Selves. Troubled Identities in a Postmodern World*, New York and Oxford: Oxford University Press, 1-20.

Haakana, Markku (1999) *Laughing Matters. A Conversation Analytical Study of Laughter in Doctor-Patient Interaction*, Department of Finnish Language. University of Helsinki.

Hakanen, Aimo (1993) 'Nesessiivisyyden ilmaisemisesta nykysuomessa' [On expressing necessity in contemporary Finnish], in *Systeemi ja poikkeama. Turun yliopiston suomalaisen ja yleisen kielitieteen julkaisuja nro 42*, Turku: University of Turku, 177-193.

Halliday, M.A.K. (1985) *An Introduction to Functional Grammar*, London: Edward Arnold.

Halverson, Sandra (2003) 'The cognitive basis of translation universals', *Target* 15(2): 197-241.

Hammersley, Martyn and Paul Atkinson (1983) *Ethnography. Principles in Practice*, London and New York: Tavistock Publications.

Hansen, Josée (2003) 'The Negotiator' (Interview of Martine Reicherts), *d'Land*, 19 December 2003, http://www.land.lu/hrtml/dossiers/dossier_siege_ue/reicherts_191203.html. Accessed 21 June 2005.

Harquail, Celia V. (1998) 'Organizational Identification and the 'Whole Person': Integrating Affect, Behavior, and Cognition', in David A. Whetten and Paul V. Godfrey (eds) *Organizational Identity. Building Theory Through Conversations*, Thousand Oaks: Sage, 223-231.

Hatch, Mary Jo (1997) 'Irony and the Social Construction of Contradiction in the Humor of a Management Team', *Organization Science* 8(3): 275-288.

------ and Stanford B. Ehrlich (1993) 'Spontaneous Humour as an Indicator of Paradox and Ambiguity in Organizations', *Organization Studies* 14(4): 505-526.

Heikkinen Vesa, Pirjo Hiidenmaa and Ulla Tiililä (2000) *Teksti työnä, virka kielenä* [Working with Texts, Languaging the Office], Helsinki: Gaudeamus.

Hermans, Theo (1999) *Translation in Systems*, Manchester: St. Jerome.

------ (2003) 'Translation and the Relevance of Self-Reference', paper given on 10 September 2003, at CETRA Summer School 2003, Scuola Superiore Traduttori Interpreti 'San Pellegrino', Misano Adriatico.

Hester, Stephen and David Francis (2001) 'Is institutional talk a phenomenon? Reflections on ethnomethodology and applied conversation analysis', in Alec McHoul and Mark Rapley (eds) *How to Analyse Talk in Institutional Settings. A Casebook of Methods*, London and New York: Continuum, 206-217.

Hogg, Michael A. and Dominic Abrams (1988) *Social Identifications. A social psychology of intergroup relations and group processes,* London and New York: Routledge.

Holmes, Janet (2000) 'Politeness, power and provocation: how humour functions in the workplace', *Discourse Studies* 2(2): 159-185.

Hooghe, Liesbet (1997) 'Serving 'Europe' – Political Orientations of Senior Commission Officials', *European Integration online Papers* 1(8), http://eiop. or.at/eiop/texte/1997-008a.htm. Accessed 7 June 2005.

------ (2005) 'Several Roads Lead to International Norms, But Few via International Socialization. A Case Study of the European Commission', *International Organization* 59(4): 861-898.

Hopper, Joseph (2001) 'Contested Selves in Divorce Proceedings', in Jaber F. Gubrium and James A. Holstein (eds) *Institutional Selves. Troubled Identities in a Postmodern World*, New York and Oxford: Oxford University Press, 127-141.

Hyland, Ken (2005) 'Stance and engagement: a model of interaction in academic discourse', *Discourse Studies* 7(2): 173-192.

Iedema, Rick (1997) 'The language of administration: organizing human activity in formal institutions', in F. Christie and J.R. Martin (eds) *Genre and Institutions. Social Processes in the Workplace and School*, London and Washington: Cassell, 73-100.

de Jong, Menno and P. J. Schellens (2000) 'Toward a Document Evaluation Methodology: What Does Research Tell Us About the Validity and Reliability of Evaluation Methods?' *IEEE Transactions on Professional Communication* 43(3): 242-260.

Karvonen, Pirjo (1996) *Suomi eurooppalaisessa kieliyhteisössä.* [Finnish in the European Language Community], Opetusministeriön koulu- ja tiedepolitiikan osaston julkaisusarja 42. Helsinki: Ministry of Education.

Kauppinen, Anneli (1998) *Puhekuviot, tilanteen ja rakenteen liitto. Tutkimus kielen omaksumisesta ja suomen konditionaalista* [Study of Language Acquisition and the Finnish Conditional], Helsinki: SKS.

Kittel, Harald (1998) 'Inclusions and Exclusions: The "Göttingen Approach" to Translation Studies and Inter-Literary History', in Kurt Mueller-Vollmer and Michael Irmscher (eds) *Translating Literatures, Translating Culture. New Vistas and Approaches in Literary Studies*, Göttinger Beiträge zur Internationalen Übersetzungsforschung, Band 17, Berlin: Erich Schmidt Verlag.

Koskinen, Kaisa (1994) '(Mis)translating the untranslatable – The impact of deconstruction and post-structuralism in translation theory', *META* 39(3): 446-452.

------ (2000a) 'Institutional Illusions. Translating in the EU Commission', *The Translator* 6 (1): 49-65.

------ (2000b) *Beyond Ambivalence. Postmodernity and the Ethics of Translation* (Diss.) Acta universitatis Tamperensis 773, Tampere: University of Tampere. http://acta.uta.fi/english/teos.phtml?4347.

------ (2001) 'Ekvivalenssista erojen leikkiin. Käännöstiede ja kääntäjän etiikka' [From equivalence to the play of differences, TS and the ethics of translation], in Pirjo Mäkinen and Riitta Oittinen (eds) *Alussa oli käännös,* Tampere: Tampere University Press, 374-387.

------ (2004) 'Shared culture? Reflections on recent trends in Translation Studies', *Target* 16(1): 143-156.

Lefevere, André (1992) *Translation, Rewriting, and the Manipulation of Literary Fame*, London and New York: Routledge.

Leinonen, Satu (2001) 'Asioimistulkkaus – paljon muutakin kuin asioimisen tulkkausta' [Community interpreting – much more than just interpreting in the community], in Riitta Oittinen and Pirjo Mäkinen (eds) *Alussa oli käännös*, Tampere: Tampere University Press, 294-304.

------ (forthcoming) *Turn-taking organization in interpreter-mediated conversations*. Dissertation. University of Tampere.

Leuven-Zwart, Kitty van (1990) 'Translation and Original: Similarities and Dissimilarities, II', *Target* 2: 69-95.

Levi-Strauss, Claude (1955) *Tristes Tropiques*, Paris: Librairie Plon.

Lönnroth, Karl-Johan (2005) 'How to ensure the total quality in a changing translation market – a European approach', in Leena Salmi and Kaisa Koskinen (eds) *Proceedings of the XVII World Congress*, Tampere: International Federation of Translators, 30-34.

------ (2007) 'It's possible to move this ship despite its size and complexity: Karl-Johan Lönnroth, Director General of DGT since 2004'. Special issue Behind the Scenes: 50 Years Translating for Europe, *DGTinfo* 518, 23 March 2007, 16-17.

Malinowski, Bronislav (1922) *Argonauts of the Western Pacific: An Account of Native Enterprise and Adventure in the Archipelagoes of Melanesian New Guinea*, London: Routledge and Kegan Paul.

Marcus, George E. (1994) 'What Comes (Just) After 'Post'? The Case of Ethnography', in Norman K. Denzin and Yvonna S. Lincoln (eds) *Handbook of Qualitative Research*, Thousand Oaks: Sage, 563-574.

Martin, Joanne (2002) *Organizational Culture. Mapping the Terrain*, Thousand Oaks: Sage.

Martin, J.R. (1997) 'Analysing Genre: Functional Parameters', in F. Christie and J.R. Martin (eds) *Genre and Institutions. Social Processes in the Workplace and School*, London and Washington: Cassell, 3-39.

Mason, Ian (2003) 'Text Parameters in Translation: Transitivity and Institutional Cultures', in Heidrun Gerzymisch-Arbogast, Eva Hajičová, Petr Sgall, Zuzana Jettmarová, Annely Rothkegel and Dorothee Rothfuss Bastian (eds) *Textologie und Translation*. (Jahrbuch Übersetzen und Dolmetschen 4/II.) Tübingen: Gunter Narr, 175-188.

Matthiessen, Christian M.I.M (2001) 'The environments of translation', in Erich Steiner and Colin Yallop (eds) *Exploring Translation and Multilingual Text Production: Beyond Content*, Berlin and New York: Mouton de Gruyter, 41-124.

McHoul, Alec and Mark Rapley (2001) 'Preface: with a little help from our friends', in Alec McHoul and Mark Rapley (eds) *How to Analyse Talk in Institutional Settings. A Casebook of Methods*, London and New York: Continuum, xi-xiv.

Merton, Robert K. (1998) 'Foreword', in Mary C. Brinton and Victor Nee (eds) *The New Institutionalism in Sociology*, Stanford: Stanford University Press, xi-xiii.

------, Marjorie Fiske and Patricia L. Kendall (1956) *The Focused Interview. A Manual of Problems and Procedures*, Glencoe, Illinois: The Free Press.

Meyerson, Debra E. (1991) "Normal Ambiguity?' A Glimpse of an Occupational Culture', in Peter J. Frost, Larry F. Moore, Meryl Reis Luis, Craig C. Lundberg and Joanne Martin (eds) *Reframing Organizational Culture*, Newbury Park: Sage, 131-156.

Morrison, David E. (2003) 'Good and Bad Practice in Focus Group Research', in Virginia Nightingale and Karen Ross (eds) *Critical Readings: Media and Audiences*, Maidenhead: Open University Press, 111-130.

Mossop, Brian (1988) 'Translating institutions: a missing factor in translation theory', *TTR* 1(2): 65-71.

------ (1990) 'Translating institutions and 'idiomatic' translation', *Meta* 35(2): 342-355.

------ (2000) 'The workplace procedures of professional translators', in Andrew Chesterman, Natividad Gallardo San Salvador and Yves Gambier (eds) *Translation in Context. Selected contributions from the EST Congress, Granada 1998*, Amsterdam and Philadelphia: John Benjamins, 39-48.

------ (2006) 'From Culture to Business. Federal Government Translation in Canada', *The Translator* 12(1): 1-27.

Munday, Jeremy (2001) *Introducing Translation Studies. Theories and Applications*, London and New York: Routledge.

Nee, Victor (1998) 'Sources of the New Institutionalism', in Mary C. Brinton and Victor Nee (eds) *The New Institutionalism in Sociology*, Stanford: Stanford University Press, 1-16.

------ and Paul Ingram (1998) 'Embeddedness and Beyond: Institutions, Exchange, and Social Structure', in Mary C. Brinton and Victor Nee (eds) *The New Institutionalism in Sociology*, Stanford: Stanford University Press, 19-45.

Nord, Christiane (1991) *Text Analysis in Translation*, Amsterdam: Rodopi.

O'Driscoll, Jim (2001) 'Hiding Your Difference: How Non-global Languages Are Being Marginalised in Everyday Interaction', *Journal of Multilingual and Multicultural Development* 22(6): 475-490.

Parsons, Talcott (1967) *The Structure of Social Action: A Study in Social Theory with Special Reference to a Group of Recent European Writers*, Glencoe, IL: Free Press.

Phillipson, Robert (2003) *English-Only Europe? Challenging Language Policy*, London and New York: Routledge.

Pöchhacker, Franz (2000) *Dolmetschen. Konzeptuelle Grundlagen und descriptive Untersuchungen* (Studien zur Translation, Vol. 7), Tübingen: Stauffenburg.

------ (2004) *Introducing Interpreting Studies*, London and New York: Routledge.

Popovič, Anton (1970) 'The Concept "Shift of Expression" in Translation Analysis', in J.S. Holmes, F. de Haan and A. Popovič (eds) *The Nature of Translation. Essays on the Theory and Practice of Literary Translation*, Haag, Paris: Mouton/Bratislava: The Publishing House of the Slovak Academy of Sciences.

Pym, Anthony (1997) *Pour une éthique du traducteur*, Artois Presses Université/ Presses de l'Université d'Ottawa.

------ (1998) *Method in Translation History,* Manchester: St. Jerome.

------ (2000) 'The European Union and its Future Languages', *Across Languages and Cultures* 1(1): 1-17.

------ (2001) 'Translation and International Institutions. Explaining the Diversity Paradox', http://www.fut.es/~apym/on-line/diversity.html. Accessed 13 February 2003.

Risku, Hanna (2004) *Translationsmanagement. Interkulturelle Fachkommunikation im Informationszeitalter*, Tübingen: Gunter Narr.

Šarčević, Susan (1997) *New Approach to Legal Translation*, The Hague: Kluwer.

Schein, Edgar H. (1991) 'What Is Culture?', in Peter J. Frost, Larry F. Moore, Meryl Reis Luis, Craig C. Lundberg and Joanne Martin (eds) *Reframing Organizational Culture*, Newbury Park: Sage, 243-253.

Schäffner, Christina (2002) 'Translation, Politics, Ideology', *CTIS Occasional Papers*, Vol. 2, Manchester, Centre for Translation Studies: UMIST, 97-111.

Schwartzman, Helen B. (1993) *Ethnography in Organizations*, Newbury Park: Sage.

Scott, W. Richard (2001) *Institutions and Organizations* (2nd ed.), Thousand Oaks: Sage.

Sharrock, Wes and John A. Hughes (2001) 'Ethnography in the workplace: Remarks on its theoretical bases', http://www.teamethno-online.org/Issue1/Wes. html. Accessed 13 January 2005.

Sidiropoulou, Maria (2004) *Linguistic Identities through Translation*, Amsterdam: Rodopi.

Silverman, David (2001) *Interpreting Qualitative Data*, London: Sage.

Silverman, Sydel (2002) 'Foreword', in Richard G. Fox and Barbara J. King (eds) *Anthropology Beyond Culture*, Oxford and New York: Berg, xv-xix.

Spivak, Gayatri Chakravorty (1999) *A Critique of Postcolonial Reason. Toward a*

History of the Vanishing Present, Cambridge and London: Harvard University Press.

Stevens, Anne (2001) *Brussels Bureaucrats? The Administration of the European Union* (with Handley Stevens), Basingstoke: Palgrave.

Sturge, Kate (1997) 'Translation Strategies in Ethnography', *The Translator* 3(1): 21-38.

------ (2007*) Representing Others: Translation, Ethnography and Museum*, Manchester: St. Jerome.

Sulkunen, Irma (1999) *Liisa Eerikintytär ja hurmosliikkeet 1700-1800-luvuilla* [Liisa Eerik's daughter and extatic movements in the 18th and 19th centuries], Helsinki: Gaudeamus.

------ (2003), 'Tutkija – maailmankuva – vakaumus' [Researcher – world view – conviction], Contribution at the the seminar 'Minun maailmani – tutkijan maailmankuva tutkimuksen lähtökohtana ja kontekstina' [My world – Researcher's world view as the starting point and context of research], Tampere: University of Tampere, Department of History, 28 November.

Suter, Elizabeth A. (2000) 'Focus Groups in Ethnography of Communication: Expanding Topics of Inquiry Beyond Participant Observation', *The Qualitative Report* 5(1-2), http://www.nova.edu.ssss/QR/QR5-1/suter.html. Accessed 8 November 2004.

Swales, John M. (1998) *Other Floors, Other Voices. A Textography of a Small University Building*, Mahwah, N.J. and London: Lawrence Erlbaum Associates.

Tomasi, Luca (2003) 'Translating Transparency in the EU Commission', in Arturo Tosi (ed.) *Crossing Barriers and Bridging Cultures: The Challenges of Multilingual Translation for the European Union*, Clevedon Hall: Multilingual Matters, 88 98.

Tosi, Arturo (2003) 'European Affairs: The Writer, the Translator and the Reader', in Arturo Tosi (ed.) *Crossing Barriers and Bridging Cultures: The Challenges of Multilingual Translation for the European Union*, Clevedon Hall: Multilingual Matters, 45-66.

------ (ed.) (2003) *Crossing Barriers and Bridging Cultures: The Challenges of Multilingual Translation for the European Union*, Clevedon Hall: Multilingual Matters.

Toury, Gideon (1995) *Descriptive Translation Studies and Beyond*, Amsterdam and Philadelphia: John Benjamins.

Trosborg, Anna (1997) 'Translating Hybrid Political Texts', in Anna Trosborg (ed.) *Text Typology and Translation*, Amsterdam and Philadelphia: John Benjamins.

Tymoczko, Maria (2002) 'Connecting the Two Infinite Models. Research Methods in Translation Research', in Theo Hermans (ed.) *Crosscultural Transgressions. Research Models in Translation Studies II*, Manchester: St. Jerome, 9-25.

Van Maanen, John (1988) *Tales of the Field. On Writing Ethnography*, Chicago and London: The University of Chicago Press.

Venuti, Lawrence (1995) *The Translator's Invisibility. A history of translation*, London and New York: Routledge.

------ (1998) *The Scandals of Translation. Towards an Ethics of Difference,* London and New York: Routledge.

Vinay, Jean-Paul and Jean Darbelnet (1958) *Stylistique Comparée du français et de l'anglais*, Paris: Didier.

Vuorikoski, Anna-Riitta (2004) *A Voice of Its Citizens or a Modern Tower of Babel? The Quality of Interpreting as a Function of Political Rhetoric in the European Parliament*, Tampere University: Acta Universitatis Tamperensis 985.

Vuorinen, Erkka (1996) *Crossing Cultural Boundaries in International News Transmission – A Translational Approach.* Unpublished licentiate thesis, Tampere: University of Tampere.

Wagner, Emma, Svend Bech and Jesús M. Martínez (2002) *Translating for the European Union Institutions*, Manchester: St. Jerome.

Weiss, Gilbert and Ruth Wodak (2000) 'Debating Europe: Globalization Rhetoric and European Union Unemployment Policies', in Irène Bellier and Thomas M. Wilson (eds) *An Anthropology of the European Union. Building, Imagining and Experiencing the New Europe*, Oxford and New York: Berg, 75-92.

Whyte, William F. (1943) *Street Corner Society. The Social Structure of an Italian Slum,* Chicago: University of Chicago Press.

Wilson, Thomas M. (2000) 'Agendas in Conflict: Nation, State and Europe in the Northern Ireland Borderlands', in Irène Bellier and Thomas M. Wilson (eds) *An Anthropology of the European Union. Building, Imagining and Experiencing the New Europe*, Oxford and New York: Berg, 137-158.

Wolf, Michaela (2002) 'Culture as Translation – and Beyond. Ethnographic Models of Representation in Translation Studies', in Theo Hermans (ed.) *Crosscultural Transgressions*, Manchester: St. Jerome, 180-192.

Wright Mills, C. (1959) *The Sociological Imagination,* New York: Oxford University Press.

Zabusky, Stacia E. (2000) 'Boundaries at Work: Discourses and Practices of Belonging in the European Space Agency', in Irène Bellier and Thomas M. Wilson (eds) *An Anthropology of the European Union. Building, Imagining and Experiencing the New Europe*, Oxford and New York: Berg, 179-200.

Index